Speaking Christ for the Building Up of the Body of Christ

Witness Lee

Living Stream Ministry
Anaheim, California

First Edition, 6,250 copies. June 1988.

Library of Congress Catalog
Card Number: 88-82030

ISBN 0-87083-421-5 (hardcover)
ISBN 0-87083-422-3 (softcover)

Published by

Living Stream Ministry
1853 W. Ball Road, Anaheim, CA 92804 U.S.A.
P. O. Box 2121, Anaheim, CA 92814 U.S.A.

Printed in the United States of America

CONTENTS

CONTENTS

PREFACE

This book is composed of messages given by Brother Witness Lee from February 22 to March 5, 1988 in a training in Irving, Texas.

CHAPTER ONE

THE SPEAKING IN OUR MEETINGS

(1)

Scripture Reading: Acts 6:10; 2 Cor. 4:13; Acts 4:31; 1 Cor. 14:26; Eph. 5:19; Col. 3:16b

Our fellowship in this book may be considered as a continuation of our fellowship from the winter training of 1987, which is contained in the book entitled *The Scriptural Way to Meet and to Serve for the Building Up of the Body of Christ*. In this book we want to see more concerning this scriptural way.

THE FOUR BASIC FACTORS AND ELEMENTS IN OUR MEETINGS— THE WORD, THE SPIRIT, PRAYING, AND SINGING

We need to learn how to practice all kinds of meetings: the home meetings, the small group meetings, and the larger meetings of the church. In all of our meetings there should be four basic factors and elements: the word, the spirit, praying, and singing. If we handle these four elements in a proper and living way, there will be a rich display and expression of Christ in all of our meetings.

The word is the holy word revealed in the Scriptures, either the constant Word or the instant word. If we are going to be the speaking ones in our meetings, we must let the word of Christ dwell in us richly (Col. 3:16). The riches of Christ are in His word. The word of the Lord must have adequate room within us that it may operate and minister these riches into our being. Then our speaking of the word in the meetings will be an exhibition of the riches of Christ.

When we refer to the spirit, we are following the Apostle Paul to denote our spirit indwelt by and mingled with the Holy Spirit. According to the New Testament, the divine

Spirit and our human spirit are mingled together as one spirit. He that is joined to the Lord, who is the Spirit, is one spirit (1 Cor. 6:17; 2 Cor. 3:17). In a regenerated person, the divine Spirit and the human spirit are no longer two separate spirits. The Spirit of the Lord and the spirit as our inward being are one spirit.

In the meetings, we need to take care of our mingled spirit. We have to learn how to exercise our spirit. Whenever we touch our spirit, use our spirit, exercise our spirit, the Spirit within our spirit immediately works. The two spirits are not only joined but also mingled as one. If two substances are mingled together and we touch one of them, we surely will touch the other one. Therefore, in our daily life and in our meeting life, we must learn how to handle, deal with, and exercise our spirit.

The divine Trinity consummates in the Spirit. The Spirit, the Holy Spirit, the Spirit of God, is the very consummation of the divine Trinity. The three of the divine Godhead needed a consummation, and this consummation was taken care of by the processes through which the Triune God passed. Incarnation is a part of the consummation of the Triune God. Before the incarnation, our God was "raw." God had to pass through incarnation to be "cooked." When groceries are cooked, they are consummated to make a meal. Before the incarnation, the Triune God—the Father, the Son, and the Spirit—was there, but He had not been cooked, or consummated. Before the incarnation, was there any humanity in the Godhead? Although our God is omniscient, He did not have the experience of human life or human living. But after His incarnation, the Triune God picked up humanity and passed through human living for thirty-three and a half years. Thirty-three and a half years of human living is a long process. Before the incarnation, there was nothing of human living contained in the Godhead. But today the Godhead contains the riches of human living.

Another process the Triune God passed through was the wonderful death of Christ. In Adam death is a terrible term, but in Christ death is very sweet. We all have to experience the death in Christ. This death was not in the Godhead before the incarnation of the Triune God and the death of Christ, the Triune God-man. But today death is included. Death is contained in the Triune God-man. The death in Adam is fully negative, but the death in Christ is wonderfully positive. It is a dear death, a lovable death. The Triune God also passed through the processes of resurrection and ascension. He was God in the heavens before His incarnation, but He had never come down from the heavens, descended to Hades, resurrected from the dead, and ascended to the highest place in the universe. The resurrection and the ascension became a part of His experience. In the Godhead today, there is the element of ascension.

Incarnation, human living, crucifixion, resurrection, and ascension are wonderful items that we should love and treasure. Don't you love incarnation? Don't you love His humanity? Don't you love His human living on this earth? He was a little babe, He was even a boy of twelve years, and He was a man of thirty-three years. Don't you love His death? Don't you treasure His resurrection? Paul wanted to know Christ and the power of His resurrection, and he was even desiring to be conformed to His death (Phil. 3:10). Do you appreciate being conformed to the death of Christ, and have you asked the Lord to conform you to His death? Instead of praying in this way, you may have prayed many religious prayers, asking the Lord to help you be holy and humble. We should tell the Lord that we want to know Him and the power of His resurrection, being conformed to His death. All these elements today are wrapped up with the divine Trinity. As His believers, we must learn how to handle all these items of the Triune God's process whenever we meet because these items are the very essences, or elements, of the consummation of the Triune God.

Before the resurrection of Christ the Triune God had never been consummated. After the resurrection, the Lord Jesus came back to His disciples and charged them to go to disciple the nations, baptizing them into the name of the

Father, the Son, and the Spirit. Why was this charge given right after His resurrection? The right time for Him to charge His disciples to baptize the new believers into the Triune God was after His resurrection because before that moment, the Triune God had not yet been completed, or consummated. In resurrection Christ, the very embodiment of the Triune God, became a life-giving Spirit. Thus, the all-inclusive, life-giving Spirit is the completion of the Triune God. The Triune God was perfect, but He was not yet completed before the resurrection of Christ. He was completed with incarnation, with human living, with the all-inclusive death of Christ, with the resurrection of Christ, and with the ascension of Christ. When the Spirit was poured out from the heavens by the ascended Christ, that Spirit was the consummation of the Triune God, the reality of the Triune God.

In the last chapter of the sixty-six books of the Bible, the Spirit is mentioned without any adjective. He is not referred to as the Holy Spirit or the Spirit of God, but as *the* Spirit (Rev. 22:17a). The Spirit, this unique Spirit, is the very consummation of the processed Triune God. This One says something together with another one in Revelation 22. The other one is the bride, the consummated humanity. The Spirit is the consummation of the Triune God, and the bride is the consummation of the tripartite mankind. After the processes they both have gone through, they both form a universal couple. The husband is the consummation of God and the wife is the consummation of man. We will be the consummated mankind as the very wife to the consummated Triune God. The record of the sixty-six books of the Bible is a record of a romance. The consummated God, the Spirit, falls in love with the consummated man.

The Spirit as the consummation of the processed God is in our spirit, in our mouth, and in our heart (Rom. 8:16; 10:8), and He will never leave us. He stays with us forever. When we say, "O Lord Jesus" or "O Father God," immediately we touch Him. When we call "O Lord Jesus" out of a pure heart, we have a sweet feeling within. When

Paul met the Lord on the road to Damascus, the Lord spoke to him, "Saul, Saul, why are you persecuting Me?" (Acts 9:4). When Paul heard this, he did not understand. He said, "Who are You, Lord?" The Lord responded, "I am Jesus, whom you are persecuting" (v. 5). He did not realize that the "Me" he was persecuting was a corporate Me, comprising Jesus the Lord and all His believers. He thought he was persecuting the followers of Jesus, not knowing that when he persecuted them, he persecuted Jesus, for they were one with Him by being united to Him through their faith in Him. After the Apostle Paul had received the Lord, Ananias told him, "Rise up and be baptized, and wash away your sins, calling on His name" (Acts 22:16). According to the Greek, "calling" is a participle as an adverb modifying "be baptized." This indicates that while Paul was being baptized he was calling on the name of the Lord. When we go to visit people and lead them to believe and be baptized, we must instruct them to call. We can say, "While I am putting you into this water, you have to call on the name of the Lord—O Lord Jesus! O Lord Jesus!" Romans 10:12 says that "the same Lord of all is rich to all who call upon Him." The Lord is rich to all the ones who call on His name.

When we call upon the Lord, we receive Him as the consummation of the Triune God, and this consummation is the Spirit. Some may consider that the Spirit as the consummation of the Triune God is so marvelous that He is beyond our understanding and apprehension. Although the Spirit is so marvelous, He is as available as the air. Our physical body lives by the air. If the air were not so available to us, we would die within a short time. The air is so great, but it is so available and even so cheap. I do not spend money for air. Wherever I go, the air follows me. Wherever I go, the air is waiting for me. Air is so great, yet the greatest thing in this universe is the most normal, the most common. Today the Bible likens the consummated God, the Spirit, to air. Everything that we enjoy of the Triune God today is miraculous yet very normal. Thus, when we come to the meeting we must know how to handle

such a normal Christian experience, that is, the exercise of
our spirit to contact the Spirit.

From 1969 to 1972 in Elden Hall in Los Angeles, the
saints practiced calling on the name of the Lord on the
way to the meetings and in the meetings, but after 1972
that practice began to disappear. Today we often come to
the meeting in a quiet way, and we are even quiet in the
meeting. We come into the meeting so quietly because we
are used to this. Why would we not call audibly on the
name of the Lord? When we were home, were we that
silent? Outside of the meeting hall we may be very
talkative and loud, but the meeting hall is a place that
silences people. Do we need to wait for somebody to speak
something, to call a hymn, to name a verse, or to read to us
in the meeting? After so many years in the Lord's recovery,
many of us still need a leading one to stand up and tell us
to read the Scriptures. This shows that speaking in the
meetings has not been built up as a habit in our spirit.

Why are we Christians today so weak? Why are our
meetings so dead and even so deadening? It is because we
are too silent. Is our God a dumb God? When Paul talks
about the Christian meeting in 1 Corinthians 14:26, he
begins from chapter twelve. In his opening word of this
chapter Paul points out that our God is not a dumb God.
Today we do not worship the dumb idols, but we worship a
speaking God (vv. 2-3). Our God is a speaking God. God has
spoken, and God is still speaking (Heb. 1:1-2). Therefore,
we must be the speaking people. We must learn to speak.

Our Christian heritage today is in two things—the
Word and the Spirit. We have the Word without and the
Spirit within, and these two are one. The Word is the Spirit
and the Spirit is the Word. When I have the Word in my
hands it is the Word outside of me, but when I pray-read
the Word, it gets into me and becomes the Spirit. When I
speak the Spirit out to you, the Spirit becomes the word,
and when you receive this word into you, it becomes the
Spirit. As I am speaking the word, you are receiving the
Spirit. But the strangest thing is this—we are supposed to
be the speaking people of the speaking God, yet we do not

speak. We need to learn how to handle the Word and the Spirit. My intention and my burden is that the saints would learn how to speak forth Christ properly, to speak in the Spirit and with the Spirit.

Another basic factor and element in our meetings is prayer. We have to learn to pray. The word and the Spirit must issue in our praying. In our meetings there should be many prayers. Many of our prayers, however, are too formal, too religious, and too legal. We may pray merely to fulfill our church responsibility. Before a certain brother was appointed as an elder, he may have hardly prayed in the church meetings. After he was appointed to be an elder, however, he came to the front row and began to pray. That is not a genuine prayer but a fulfilling of duty as an elder. We need to forget about that kind of formal, official, duty-fulfilling prayer. I have known some saints in the past who have criticized others for praying three or four times in the meeting. These ones were critical, yet they themselves did not pray at all in the meeting. Actually, our church meetings need to be full of spontaneous and living prayers. We offer too many religious, duty-fulfilling prayers. Our prayers are not that spontaneous, real, genuine, or true. They are not that much in our spirit. We should not plan what to pray ahead of time. Our prayers should come out of us spontaneously in the way that we breathe. Our meetings are dead because we are short of these living, spontaneous prayers.

Another basic factor and element in our meetings is singing. Both speaking and singing are the issue of the infilling of our spirit. If we are filled in our spirit something will flow out of us in speaking and singing. In Ephesians 5:18-19, Paul tells us to "be filled in spirit, speaking to one another in psalms and hymns and spiritual songs, singing and psalming with your heart to the Lord." Colossians 3:16, a sister verse to Ephesians 5:19, says, "Let the word of Christ dwell in you richly, in all wisdom teaching and admonishing one another in psalms, hymns, and spiritual songs, singing with grace in your hearts to God." The issue of our allowing the word to fill us is speaking and singing. Psalms, hymns, and spiritual songs are more for speaking than for singing. In our present practice, we mostly sing the hymns. We have not built up a habit of speaking the hymns to one another. We must learn to speak the hymns. Some of us fall into formality with our singing. Others sing crazily. But where is the real singing with the spirit and with the mind (1 Cor. 14:15)? We must exercise our regenerated spirit with our renewed mind in singing to the Lord. Our meetings are short of the word, the spirit, praying, and singing.

THE SPEAKING IN OUR MEETINGS

The speaking in our meetings should be with the Spirit (Acts 6:10). To speak with the Spirit is to exercise our spirit. When we exercise our spirit the Spirit is present. We do not need to wait for the Spirit to descend upon us because the Spirit is in our spirit, in our mouth, and in our heart. According to Romans 10:8, the Spirit as the word is even in the mouth and the heart of an unbeliever as he hears the gospel being preached. If an unbeliever is going to receive the Lord, to retain Him, he has to say, "O Lord Jesus." Once he calls on the Lord, the Lord as the Spirit comes into his spirit and will never leave him. We need to speak with the Spirit by exercising our spirit.

We also need to speak by our spirit mingled with the Spirit (2 Cor. 4:13a and note 2). According to 2 Corinthians 4:13 our mingled spirit by which we speak is a spirit of faith. Both Dean Alford and M. R. Vincent indicate in their writings that the spirit here is not merely the Holy Spirit but our spirit mingled with the Holy Spirit. When we speak the word of the Lord by our spirit we surely will have faith. We need to speak in faith. When we speak in faith, we will speak with boldness (Acts 4:31). Boldness is a kind of assurance, and the assurance comes from our faith. Without faith we do not have any assurance and our boldness is gone. If we have faith, we have the assurance; then we have the boldness. These four items— the Spirit, our spirit, faith, and boldness—are needed for our speaking.

Some saints have been in the Lord's recovery for many years, but they have never had any change in the meeting. It seems that they will never change because they have not only made up their mind but also their disposition not to change. When they do speak, there is no mingled spirit, no faith, no assurance, and no boldness. Whether or not these saints would have a change depends on themselves. Have you ever shouted in a joyful way in the meetings? Perhaps you want to keep the status of a "lady" or a "gentleman." In the church, however, we are brothers and sisters. Brothers and sisters should be "crazy ones," ones who are excited in the spirit about their Lord whom they love.

THE WORD SPOKEN IN OUR MEETINGS

Whatever we speak in the meetings must be with Christ and the church as the center. Our speaking should not be centered on doctrines such as foot-washing or head covering. We need to take Christ, the Head, with His Body, the church, as the very center of our speaking. Regardless what word we speak, the center must be Christ with the church.

The first thing, according to my study of the New Testament, that we Christians should speak in our meetings is stated in 1 Corinthians 14:26, which says, "Whenever you come together, each one has a psalm." A psalm is long and very cultured. A psalm cannot be spoken or sung in a wild, coarse, or rough way. A psalm such as Psalm 119, composed of one hundred seventy-six verses, would have to be spoken or sung in a very cultured way. When I read 1 Corinthians 14:26 in the past, I only understood that a psalm was for psalming, for singing. But the psalm mentioned in 1 Corinthians 14:26 is not merely for singing in the meetings but for speaking. According to Ephesians 5:19, when you are filled in your spirit, you speak in psalms, hymns, and spiritual songs. Psalms, hymns, and spiritual songs are poems. Psalms are the longest, hymns are shorter, and spiritual songs are the shortest. Colossians 3:16 tells us that psalms, hymns, and spiritual songs are even for teaching and admonishing.

These three verses—1 Corinthians 14:26, Ephesians 5:19,
and Colossians 3:16—are printed in our New Testament in
black and white. We may have read them a number of
times, but have we ever paid any attention to the speaking
of psalms?

In today's Christian meetings, we mostly use the New
Testament. But when Paul wrote 1 Corinthians 14:26, there
was no New Testament as we know it. What they had was
mostly the Old Testament. In the ancient times, the time of
the first apostles, although the Christians did not have the
New Testament, they had many new psalms, hymns, and
songs written according to the apostles' teaching. First
Timothy 3:16 was probably a quotation of a short song
that was very popular in the apostles' time. When they met
together, they used these psalms, hymns, and songs very
much. Some teachers would say that psalms also refer to
the old psalms in the Old Testament. I do not disagree with
this, but I believe they used more psalms, hymns, and
songs written according to the apostles' teaching for the
purpose of meeting. I am very thankful to God that we
have a New Testament and a hymnal. Our hymnal is very
good for speaking.

We need to learn to speak the stanzas of the hymns in
our hymnal. Hymn #539, "O Lord, Thou art the Spirit," is
an excellent hymn for speaking to one another. I enjoy
singing this hymn, but we also must learn to speak it. The
first two words of this hymn—"O Lord"—will stir up the
meeting. Suppose a young brother comes into a meeting in
which everybody is silent and says, "O Lord! Let's turn
to #539." Do not call the number first, but say "O Lord"
first. If we are apt to do this, when I say "O Lord," you will
say, "Thou art in me as life." Learn to speak a complete
sentence, a complete clause, or a complete expression. A
brother may stand up and say, "Brothers and sisters,
listen. The Lord to me is as life." Then someone else or
everyone together could say, "And everything to me."
Then some sisters may say together, "Me too!" Speaking
the hymns to one another is not the same as reading them.
When we speak the hymns to one another, we will taste

and see the riches of Christ in them. Sometimes you have to explain a little as you are speaking your way through a hymn. The third line of the first stanza of #539 says, "Subjective and available." A brother may say, "The Lord is not only objective but also subjective and available." Then someone else could say, "Hallelujah! The Lord is available!"

Everyone can speak the hymns in this way. We should not take the way of the clergy-laity system. In this system, the so-called laymen do not know how to speak. Only the clergyman who has studied theology and learned to speak is the one who speaks. This system builds up a hierarchy, and we must hate and repudiate it (Rev. 2:6). We must overthrow this system by exercising our spirit to speak. When we practice speaking, we need to be like a team of basketball players. We need to learn how to pass the ball and how to receive it. We all have to learn the speaking of the hymns in small meetings of six to ten. When we speak the hymns, we should speak them in a proper sequence. When someone is speaking a verse from a hymn, there should not be other competing voices. When one speaks, you should either listen to him or join him. You may wait for him to finish his speaking and then continue. Sometimes while we are speaking, we may make a noise because everyone is praising or speaking at the same time, but this should not be frequent in our meetings. Too much noise will kill the meetings. Mostly, people like to hear a clear speaking. This requires much practice. Athletes perform seemingly difficult tasks through practice, and we need to be the same as they are.

With a small number it may be easier to practice speaking the hymns. Keep a good sequence, and keep your spirit living, exercised, and released. We are so raw to this new way. But I believe that if we practice day after day, we will pick up something. Spontaneously we will be adjusted. We will adjust ourselves by practicing.

The hymns are especially rich in life experience and in truth. The poetic language is so pure. In our ordinary speaking none of us can utter the purified words that are in the hymns. This is because the hymnal was written with much consideration. Hymn #501 has seven verses. If we read and speak it to one another, we will see the riches. If we speak properly, we can render a message by our speaking. We should learn to use complete clauses, phrases, or expressions in our speaking and speak so that others can follow our speaking.

We need to learn to speak the hymns in many ways. Sometimes we need to repeat and stress. In the chorus of hymn #501 there is the phrase, "Inexhaustible, rich, and sweet!" We need to read this phrase by stressing it and by repeating it. We all have to learn to stay away from our natural way, that is, our natural reading and our natural hearing. We need to learn something new according to the Scriptures. Do not speak too loud, too low, too fast, or too slow. Exercise to speak like an expert. A person who takes piano lessons from a teacher and who practices frequently will eventually be able to play the piano properly.

The Word reveals that we need to speak the psalms, the hymns, and the spiritual songs. Surely this must be very profitable to the Christian meeting. Otherwise, the Apostle Paul would not have taught us in this way. He taught us to speak the poems, that is, the psalms, the hymns, and the spiritual songs. In three portions of the Bible—1 Corinthians 14, Ephesians 5, and Colossians 3—he taught the same thing. In the meetings of the early church, there was such a practice which was lost by Christianity. Thank God there is one book in the whole universe that still remains with us and that we can read day by day. But the tragedy is this—when we come to the Word, we always like to pick up the things that fit our natural feeling or our natural thought. Anything that is new or strange to our understanding we put aside. Year after year we read the same thing, but we hardly pick up anything.

For a foreign family to change their native, family language is not so easy. But if they have a heart to change it, they can do it. Once the language has been founded in their home, the new children do not think the language is hard to learn. They will just follow the other family members to speak the new language. By listening to the family talk, they spontaneously pick up the language. Today we are the "foreigners," who do not have this "language." When we try to speak it, we may make many mistakes. Now we must learn to speak, not in a formal way but in a living way. We need to be free in our speaking but not wild. This needs our learning and practice. I believe that if you practice speaking the hymns in groups of six to ten, you will spontaneously find out how to speak the hymns.

To have one speaker with all the others listening is not the biblical way or the Lord's ordained way for the Christian meetings. The Lord's ordained way is that all the attendants in the meeting speak. The saints at the Apostle Paul's time were not born into the habit of speaking. I believe they needed to practice. We also have to learn, and we must be faithful to endeavor in this practice. Then we will have something along this line built up in our meetings. When the newly saved ones come to the meeting, it will be very easy for them to learn this way. I began to learn the English language about seventy years ago, but my grandchildren all speak better English than I do. They have picked it up spontaneously from their English-speaking environment. We do not have a pattern of everyone speaking in our meetings today. Our pattern is to come to the meeting to be silent, waiting for somebody to call a hymn, to pray a duty-fulfilling prayer, to give a testimony, or to give an exhortation. This has become our way, our habit. Now we have to tear down and discard this way by building up another habit.

Some have said that what I have been speaking the past three years regarding the new way is correct and scriptural, but they said that they did not believe it could be worked out. If we do not work, of course, how can it be worked out? In 1958, I was staying with a group of Christians in London. One day they jested with each other about the endeavor of the United States to put a man on the moon. None of them thought the Americans could make it to the moon. About eleven years later, the United

States did put someone on the moon. They did this by endeavoring. I do not think having the proper meeting is as hard as landing on the moon. When Columbus was sailing toward America, he encountered many adversities, especially from his crew, but he exhorted his crew by saying, "Sail on! Sail on!" Eventually, he arrived at America. We also need to be those who sail on, who endeavor to enter into the scriptural way of meeting with all speaking in mutuality. The traditional way of meeting is too old and too natural, so we must drop the old way and mean business to pick up the new way and practice it. We can make it with patience and with much practice.

ENDEAVORING TO PRACTICE THE SCRIPTURAL WAY FOR THE BUILDING UP OF THE BODY OF CHRIST

Now we are endeavoring, and we are desperate because we are in the Lord's recovery. We have the riches, yet where are the people? What is the way for us to get people? Christianity has their own way, but we do not believe that is the best. By going forth to visit people, knocking on their doors, we have the assurance we can get some people. After you knock on twenty doors, you will get one. If each of us goes out to visit people with the gospel four times a year, we can gain enough new ones for us to labor on year round. After a whole year, you may still have one or two that remain. In one year, we can all gain at least one new one as remaining fruit. In this way the churches can double year after year.

We feel that we have found a scientific and definite way to keep people as remaining fruit. The way to keep people is to take care of our meeting, and the best way to take care of our meeting is by speaking. The Christian meeting is a matter of speaking. In the meetings of Christianity, there is only "one-way speaking"; there is no two-way traffic. Now we do not only have two-way traffic, but we also have multiplied ways of mutual speaking to one another.

We need to be trained to speak. We have been meeting for years and years according to a traditional and natural way. This kind of meeting is what we have seen and what we are accustomed to. But we would drop that way and come back to the biblical way. We do not have the habit of speaking, so we may not have much ability either. This is why we need to endeavor desperately to build up another habit. In the Lord's recovery, there should not be anything old or natural. Everything should be recovered according to the standard of the Bible.

I am so grateful to the Lord for the Bible. Suppose today that we did not have the Bible on this earth; in what kind of age would we be living? We would not know where to go. But thank the Lord we do have the Bible as our standard, and we know where to go. Thank the Lord that some of the saints among us have been laboring on the Word year after year; we have a history of studying the Word for over sixty years and we have reaped a lot of riches. We have put many of these riches into print. Although we have these riches, we do not have the adequate increase. Our number is too small. Thousands and thousands of people have never heard the gospel or the truths we have seen. I will never leave the central lane of Christ and the church, but I am not satisfied with the present situation. We should not take any excuse. We must learn to repudiate our present practice because it did not bring in the results. We have to repudiate it with the new way, and we have a book, the Bible, to show us the way. The only thing that is needed is our sincerity in practice. We should have a heart to practice the new way.

It is altogether worthwhile for us to endeavor to get into the new and scriptural way of meeting and serving, especially for those of us who have been in the recovery for a number of years. Even though I am an elderly brother, I am still learning. All of us can learn much more. The Spanish-speaking saints have to improve their way of speaking so that they may build up the Christian meetings according to the holy Word, making them fresh, living, refreshing, and releasing so that they will attract people to come. We will gain people, and we will have a way to keep them and build them up. Then there will be the possibility for the Lord to build up His Body as an organism for the real expression of the Triune God. Today on this earth, we can see "churches," but we cannot see a living Body as an organism of the Triune God. There is not such a thing on this earth yet. There are millions of Christians, but where is this organism? Where is the Body of Christ built? For this we must endeavor.

Our present situation forced us to come back to the holy Word to find out something concerning the Lord's way. I believe the Lord has shown us His way to gain people and to build up His Body. Whether or not this will work depends upon how much we will endeavor, how much we will labor, how much we will really offer ourselves to the Lord's new way. If there is a will, there is a way. I would especially encourage all of us to practice speaking the hymns. A group of six to ten saints can gather together and practice speaking the hymns. In addition to speaking these poems in our meetings, we also need to speak teachings, revelations (1 Cor. 14:26), the gospel (Acts 5:42), and personal testimonies (cf. Acts 15:12). We need to learn how to speak in all these ways in our meetings that they may be enriched, living, and attractive.

THE SPEAKING IN OUR MEETINGS

(2)

Scripture Reading: 1 Cor. 14:26; Acts 5:42; 1 Cor. 2:10; Acts 2:42; 1 Tim. 1:3-4

TEACHINGS

In chapter one we have seen that the word spoken in our meetings includes poems such as psalms, hymns, and spiritual songs. First Corinthians 14:26 and Acts 5:42 tell us that teachings should also be spoken in our meetings. These teachings, of course, must be according to the unique teaching of the apostles, and they are concerning the Triune God, concerning Christ, concerning the Spirit, concerning the church, concerning life, concerning the Christian life, and concerning other things related to the Christian life. These are the items we should cover in our speaking as teachings. The teaching of a teacher is to minister the riches of Christ to edify and nourish others.

In the Lord's new way, each one of us has to learn to speak more than a few sentences. We have to be trained by the Lord and prepared in the Spirit to give a message. In one meeting we may have a burden and be led by the Spirit to speak a message for about three minutes concerning one of the major points in the Bible. To speak in this way, we have to learn much.

REVELATIONS, THE GOSPEL, AND PERSONAL TESTIMONIES

According to 1 Corinthians 14:26, we also need to speak forth revelations in our meetings. Teachings are the word mainly of our understanding; revelations are the word mainly of our spirit, and they are concerning the deep things of Christ (1 Cor. 2:10 and note 3). The gospel for the unsaved and for the newly saved (Acts 5:42) and personal testimonies (cf. Acts 15:12) should also be spoken in our meetings. What we speak should always be within the limit of the teaching of the apostles (Acts 2:42), avoiding anything other than God's economy (1 Tim. 1:3-4).

LEARNING TO SPEAK
IN A PROPER WAY IN THE MEETINGS
TO BUILD UP THE BODY OF CHRIST

You should not speak too low or too loud, too slow or too fast. First, you have to learn to speak in a proper way so that people can hear you clearly. Once, Brother Nee charged us not to love our throat, but to take care of the listeners. On the other hand, shouting cuts off the clarity of the spoken word. We need to speak loudly so that people can hear us, but speaking too loudly will make the words unclear. To speak too quickly will confuse the audience, whereas to speak too slowly will exhaust the audience's patience. Another important point is that when we speak a message, we must speak every point with every aspect so accurately. Because we are human, we easily make mistakes. Yet we must try to speak things correctly and accurately. Through a careful study of the Word, the Lord will enable us to share the points of a message accurately.

We also need to learn to speak corporately in a distinct and clear way. A clear voice is not only for God but also for man to listen to. Only God can fully understand a noise. To avoid making an unintelligible noise all the time, we must learn to coordinate with others in the meeting. This is similar to the way a good driver drives his car. He not only takes care of the car he is driving but also is aware of the other cars around him so that he can avoid having an accident. While we are speaking, we must exercise our hearing to listen to others. When someone else is speaking, we should wait. Do not speak in a noisy way. Always speak with a clear voice.

In the New Testament, especially in 1 Corinthians 14, the apostle not only charged us to speak but also instructed us how to speak. If you read 1 Corinthians 14 carefully, you can see some instruction there concerning our speaking in the meetings. God's ordained way for our meeting is not to have one ordained clergyman, but to have God's economy ministered by all the members in the meeting. Ephesians 4:16 says, "Out from whom all the Body, fitted and knit together through every joint of the supply, according to the operation in measure of each one part, causes the growth of the Body unto the building up of itself in love." If we are not in a meeting, how could we have the operation in measure of each one part? It is impossible. To have this kind of operation in measure of each one part and to have every joint of the supply, we surely need the meetings. When we come together to meet, this will be an occasion that affords us many opportunities to function. If you are a joint, you have the opportunity to supply the entire Body of Christ in the meeting. Also, each one part has an equal chance to minister something to the entire Body according to his operation in his particular function.

We have not seen much of this practice in the past history of the church. We have not seen Ephesians 4:16 worked out in the experience of the Lord's children. But now we have been adjusted by the Lord to be brought fully into the scriptural way of meeting and serving for the building up of the Body of Christ. He has revealed to us His way to build up not just a so-called church as an organization but to build up a living Body, a living organism. This kind of building of a living organism surely needs a meeting with all the saints functioning in speaking. I hope that those of us who are not used to speaking in the meetings would stand against our dispositions and learn how to speak. If you like to save your face, you need to go to the cross. We should not be spectators in the meetings. All the spectators should go to the cross.

Some may not have the faith that the biblical way can be worked out. For us to be brought to salvation required little work on our part. The Lord did everything for us. We just believed in Him and called on Him to receive Him. But for us to carry out God's economy in our speaking in the meetings is very difficult. Sometimes I thought that some people were born in the way that they could never speak publicly. If you ask some people to speak in a public meeting, you will kill them. They cannot make it. In the past I wondered whether or not this kind of member would be able to speak, but now I believe that even this kind of member can speak. In the long run, they will learn to speak. The Spirit has a way.

We should not forget that we have two marvelous gifts—the Spirit and the Word. The Spirit is within us. We have such a Spirit as a living, capable, and able Teacher within us. I am so grateful to the Lord that we also have the Bible. Whatever He has spoken has been written down and printed. We have God's Word, His "textbook," in our hand, and we have a Teacher in our spirit. Surely what this Teacher can do is much, much better than what any person can do. He can teach us inwardly and lead us into the reality of His Word. Regardless of how inadequate we are, if we have the heart to seek after Him, He will teach us to speak. Eventually, we will be able to speak for three minutes on some major truths in God's economy. Probably at first the Spirit will lead us and teach us to give a testimony. We may learn how to relate our salvation experience to people. Gradually, the Spirit will lead us to speak a few verses from the Bible. Eventually, we will be raised up to be proper speaking ones for the Lord's interest.

We all have to change our concept. We should not think that certain believers cannot speak in the meeting. This is a lie from the liar, Satan. We should not believe this. We have to exercise our spirit of faith to believe that every believer can speak if he or she would speak. Do not think that the Lord's biblical way is not workable. This is a lie. We must repudiate this lie. We need to tell God's enemy, "Satan, we will believe that whatever God says in the Bible is workable. His words will never pass away though the heaven and the earth pass away" (Matt. 24:35).

What we have been fellowshipping concerning the scriptural way to meet and to serve is in the printed holy Word. These words surely will be fulfilled sooner or later. If they are not fulfilled in our time, they will be fulfilled in another time. God is faithful. We believe that every word out of His divine mouth will be fulfilled. For His word to be fulfilled, He needs us to be faithful in cooperating with Him. We need to offer ourselves to Him. We should offer our spirit, our heart, and our mind with our speaking.

You may not know what it is to exercise your spirit. If this is the case, just speak by your mind; gradually your speaking will turn from your mind to your spirit. Many of us have experienced this in prayer. When we start to pray, we may begin our prayer merely in our mind. Then as we pray on, our prayer turns from our mind to the spirit. In the same way, we must learn to speak. Do not be afraid to be exposed. Do not care for your face. It is glorious to be exposed, not shameful. If we make some mistake in the meeting by endeavoring to cooperate with the Lord in functioning, this is glorious. When we get exposed, we find out where we are, who we are, and how we need to be adjusted. Then we can progress in life and be perfected in our function. This is glorious. Are you afraid to be exposed? Blessed are those who are not afraid to be exposed in the meetings. Blessed are those who are happy to be adjusted. We all must learn to be adjusted. When we speak, we receive the light, and we are the first ones who receive the benefit.

CHAPTER THREE

THE SPEAKING IN OUR MEETINGS

(3)

Scripture Reading: John 21:15, 17; Rev. 3:1-2; 2:7, 17;
3:20-21; 1 John 1:6; 2 Cor. 13:14; 1 Thes. 5:17; Col. 4:2;
1 Tim. 2:8; Psa. 119:147-148; Gal. 5:16; Rom. 8:4; Phil. 1:19-21;
Gal. 2:20

In this chapter, we want to fellowship concerning a
very subjective matter, that is, the speaking ones in our
meetings. To speak in the meetings is really today's
problem among the Christians. The Christians who are in
the denominations have hardly any idea about the matter
of speaking in their services because they are used to
coming to these services not to speak. They were trained
this way, built up this way, raised up this way, and made a
person in this way. When they go to their church services,
they have no thought or idea about speaking in them.
Today on this earth among all the Christians, where is the
mutuality in speaking? No one gets prepared to give a
word in the meeting except for the clergy, the ones who
have been appointed to speak. Everyone has a strong
thought that to go to the church service is to listen to a
pastor or a minister speak. This is the habit. This is not
only the practice among most of the Lord's children, but
this is also something built up in their blood. This
terrifying matter still remains in our blood.

Many of us have been in the Lord's recovery for ten or
more years. Since we came into the church life and have
been meeting with the saints in the church life, we have
been attending the church meetings every week. We are the
regular ones in the church meetings, the faithful ones. We
attend the meetings as much as we can, and we have never
missed one meeting intentionally. If you have been such a
person in the recovery, attending about three meetings a

week, you have attended about one hundred fifty-six meetings a year and fifteen hundred sixty meetings in ten years. When you attended all these meetings, how many times did you get yourself prepared to speak? I would even ask how many times you thought about speaking in these meetings. In this matter, most of us must admit that we are "birds of the same feather." Whether we have been in the church life for ten years or just for one month, most of us do not have the thought of getting ourselves prepared to go to the meetings to speak. If none of us have this thought, then who is going to speak in the meeting? We say we have left the denominations, but the practice, the habit, of the denominations still follows us and even remains in us.

We must endeavor to have church meetings with many speaking and without speaking by only one person. Some of us, however, still like to be spectators in the meetings. All of us should get ourselves prepared to speak in any meeting that we attend. Although we may have been Christians for many years, we do not have the thought that we need to rise up to be the speaking ones in the meetings. The way of meeting with one person speaking and the rest listening is an annulling way.

Recently some leaders of certain denominations in the United States gathered together to talk about how to evangelize the entire world by the year 2000. Their conclusion was that they did not have enough manpower. How can they say that they have no manpower when they have millions of members? One denomination alone in the United States has approximately fourteen million members. In spite of so many people, they do not have the manpower. Where are all these people? Nearly everyone's function was killed by the way of Christianity. If only ten percent of the fourteen million members of that certain denomination were living and functioning members, these one million four hundred thousand could turn the world upside down (Acts 17:6).

The practice of Christianity has annulled the functions of the members of the Body of Christ and has choked them.

This practice has delayed the Lord's return. Why has the Lord been waiting for the past nineteen hundred years? He is still waiting. The night is darker, and there is hardly any sign among the Lord's children that the day of His appearing is going to dawn. This is because of the deadening, choking, and annulling practice which is according to the traditional way of today's Christianity. This practice crept into the Lord's recovery, and it is still here in us in a hidden way. We must take the Lord's new way, the scriptural way, of meeting and serving. The churches and the saints who have taken the scriptural way and practiced it with no opinion have gained the increase and have been revived. This is because they are simple. The cleverness of the complicated people is killing.

The trouble today is that the denominational blood still remains in our person. We have the habit of doing things according to the traditional way. To some of us it may seem terrible not to have a meeting on the Lord's Day with a good speaker speaking to us. Some may not be so happy with the change of our way. But we must realize that the truth overcomes. Nothing in this universe can do anything against the truth. We need to labor in the scriptural way with endurance. For us to have a full success in this new way may take five years, ten years, fifteen years, twenty years, thirty years, or even fifty years. Eventually, what we have been speaking concerning the scriptural way of meeting and serving for the building up of the Body of Christ will be very prevailing on this earth. The Lord has to fulfill His word. He has to do something on this earth, not to build up Christianity as a kind of "church," an organization, but to build up His Body as an organism. This can only be done by the new way that the Lord has shown us.

There are basically two ways we can take for our meeting life. One way is for us to have a pastor, or a minister, speak to us every Sunday morning. Another way is for all of us to speak in the meetings. Which way is better? We all know which way is better because we have tasted it to a certain extent. If the way of everyone speaking is better, then we must desperately endeavor to build up a habit of speaking in every meeting. The way of everyone speaking is undoubtedly better, but this way depends on something. Gold is obviously better than copper, but our possessing of gold depends upon whether we would pay the price or not. Sometimes I did not want to spend that much money for a pen, so I bought some inferior ones. After a short time, these pens were no longer any good. One day one of my relatives gave me a very good pen as a gift, and I have been using it for about seven years. I could have had such a pen in the past, but that depended upon whether or not I would pay the price. Would we pay the price to practice the new way? To hire a good speaker and listen to him speak is easy to practice. There is nothing required of us. But for us to be the speaking ones in our meetings involves at least seventeen "musts." In this chapter we will cover the first eight. We should pay the price to take the way of all of us being the speaking ones in our meetings. But would we pay the price? It is not a matter of whether or not we could pay but of whether or not we would pay the price.

It is much easier to establish a religious organization than it is to build up the church as a living organism. To establish an organization we must first raise up enough funds to rent or build a meeting place. Then we need to hire a pastor, or someone with an official degree. After we do this, we basically do not need to do anything else. We are only required to attend one or a few services and give some of our income. Then we can go back home to live the way we desire. On the next Sunday, we will come again to listen to a good speaker. This is the way in today's Christianity, but this is not the God-ordained way, the biblical way. It is the way according to tradition, the way according to the customs of the nations, the way that fits man's fallen condition. This denominational way does not need us to be revived nor does it require any kind of church life. To walk in the traditional way, the denominational way, there is no need for us to be persons who pray or who love the Lord. This way of meeting and serving fits man's natural and fallen condition.

LOVING THE LORD

For the God-ordained way, the biblical way, the new way, we all need, first of all, to love the Lord. In John 21 the Lord asked Peter if he loved Him. Peter told the Lord, "You know that I love You." Then the Lord answered, "Feed My lambs," and "Feed My sheep" (vv. 15, 17). To speak is not only to edify or to teach but also to feed the lambs and to feed the sheep. If we are going to feed the Lord's sheep, we have to speak. Without speaking, how could we feed any Christian? For us to feed the Lord's sheep, we must love Him. We should tell the Lord, "Lord, I love You, so I like to speak You forth to others." The more that we love Him, the more we are qualified, equipped, and even perfected to speak.

According to the Scriptures, the sisters are weaker vessels according to their nature by birth (1 Pet. 3:7). This is according to God's creation. But as long as the sisters love Him, they will speak. I was born in Christianity, and I was raised there for nineteen years without receiving the Lord as my Savior. But one day a young lady came to my hometown. I was nineteen years old, and she was twenty-five. That was over sixty years ago in conservative mainland China. For a young lady to speak to a thousand people was a very unique and unusual event. Although I had been to Christian meetings quite often, I went to this meeting full of curiosity to see this young lady speak. In my whole life, even up to today, I never heard a person speaking with that much authority. She was a young girl standing on the platform in a meeting place that was filled with about one thousand people. As I listened to her, all my curiosity was taken away. Every word that she spoke caught me, and I was fully convinced. I was a young man raised up in Christianity, but that day I was convinced and caught by the Lord. After the meeting as I was walking home, I prayed and gave my entire life to the Lord.

That young lady, who was only twenty-five years old, loved the Lord to the uttermost. That was her motive. Her love for the Lord was the factor, the element, and the very basic essence of her being powerful. The message she released was from the book of Exodus. She told the audience that Egypt typified the world and that all the worldly people were under the tyranny of Satan just as the children of Israel were under the tyranny of Pharaoh. She said that we had to be delivered out of this tyranny and that this was our exodus. When I heard this near the beginning of her message, I said to myself that I would not be under Satan's tyranny any more. Because this young sister loved the Lord to the uttermost, she had the Lord's authority, and the impact was in her gospel preaching.

If we love the Lord, we surely will be filled with Him. Whatever fills us within will come out of us. The overflow comes from the infilling. When we love the Lord, He will fill us. From that day in 1925 when I gave my life to the Lord, I loved to study the Bible and to talk to people about Jesus. Because I was filled with the Lord Jesus, I wanted to speak the Lord Jesus. If we are filled with the Lord Jesus, we surely will have something to pour out. If the sisters love the Lord, they will not be able to restrain themselves from speaking forth the Lord. When we love the Lord to the uttermost, we must speak. We must release the One who has filled us within.

BEING REVIVED

As we are loving the Lord, we will be revived. According to the book of Revelation, both the church in Sardis and the church in Laodicea were backsliding churches (3:1-2, 15-17). The Lord Jesus said to Sardis, "You have a name that you are living, and you are dead." Whatever the church in Sardis had was not growing but dying. They needed to repent. They needed a revival. Laodicea had become lukewarm. Because the saints of Laodicea were neither hot nor cold but lukewarm, the Lord was about to vomit them out of His mouth. They needed to repent. They needed a revival. The churches in the Lord's recovery need a revival to be brought out of such a lukewarm and dying situation.

Before we began to visit people for the gospel, the churches did not baptize that many. But since we began to take the Lord's way of visiting people to bring the gospel to them, we have baptized thirty-eight thousand people in less than two years in Taipei alone. By 1984 our situation was not encouraging. We hardly had any sensation that we were so dormant, so lukewarm, so dying, and even so deadening toward others. The number of churches was increasing through the publications of the ministry, but in general the membership in each local church was at a standstill. Most of the churches had very little increase. Why should we remain in such a dormant situation without any sensation that we have to wake up, to rise up, and to be revived? We all need a revival. Once we are revived, we will not be able to stay at home and be silent. We will have a desire to go fishing for men and to go to the homes where the fish are (Matt. 4:19). If we are going to set up a denomination, we do not need a revival. But to have a local church in the Lord's recovery that is living and prevailing with everyone speaking, we all need to be revived.

LIVING A VICTORIOUS LIFE

Then we need to live a victorious life to overcome sin, to overcome the world, to overcome ourselves, to overcome our flesh, and even to overcome our quarreling with our spouse. The wives and the husbands among us may not be so one. Many couples may not have prayed together for three years. This is the situation that really needs a revival that we may live a victorious life. In each of the seven epistles to the seven churches in Revelation 2 and 3, the closing word is that we have to overcome (2:7, 11, 17, 26; 3:5, 12, 20-21). We need an overcoming life.

ABIDING IN THE FELLOWSHIP WITH THE LORD
DAILY AND HOURLY

We also must abide in the fellowship with the Lord daily and hourly (1 John 1:6; 2 Cor. 13:14). Even the angels should be able to testify that we are in the fellowship with the Lord. We should not be away from Him but present in His fellowship. There should be no absence in our

fellowship with the Lord. Daily and even hourly we need to
be such persons. If I were not such a person, it would be
hard for me to speak in the Lord's ministry. My speaking
depends upon my continual and present fellowship with
the Lord. Why can we not speak in the meetings? Maybe
we have been absent from the Lord's fellowship for three
days because we had a quarrel with our spouse. Because of
this quarrel, we have been put away from the Lord's
fellowship. If we are going to speak for the Lord, we have
to recover our fellowship with Him by confessing our sin
and by making an apology to our spouse. We must remain,
abide, in the constant and continual fellowship with the
Lord. This is a strong demand.

BEING A PRAYING PERSON

We must also be praying persons. We should pray
unceasingly all the day long. This means that we have to
call on His name. We need to call, "O Lord." Do not think
that such a short calling means nothing. It means a lot.
While we are working in an office, teaching a class, or
doing any task, we can call, "O Lord Jesus." Such a short
calling means a lot to our Christian life. By calling on the
name of the Lord, we can pray unceasingly. For us to be
the speaking ones in our meetings we must be praying
persons.

ENJOYING THE LORD IN THE WORD
EARLY IN THE MORNING
TO HAVE A NEW START OF EACH DAY

We also must enjoy the Lord in the Word every day
early in the morning to have a new start of each day (Psa.
119:147-148). According to God's principle in His creation,
He ordained to have a new year, a new month or a new
moon, and a new day. Within every year we can have three
hundred sixty-five new starts. If we failed for three
hundred sixty-four days, we still have one more opportunity
to have a successful day. We may have failed today, but
thank the Lord tomorrow is still here waiting for us.
Tomorrow morning we will have another chance to have a

new start. Within every twenty-four hours, there is a new chance for us to have a new start and be renewed.

To have a new start is not hard. It is so easy. Just rise up a little earlier and say, "O Lord Jesus. O Lord Jesus." You do not need to shout loudly to bother others. Just say, "O Lord Jesus." To say this makes a big difference. Sometimes I forgot to call on the Lord immediately after I woke up. That became a big loss to me. As soon as I realized this I said, "Lord Jesus, forgive me for forgetting You."

Then we need to pray-read a short portion of the Word, anywhere from two to four verses. We can enjoy the Lord with His Word and in His Word through pray-reading. We should do this every day in the morning to have a good, new start. We can speak the Word to ourselves, to the Lord, and even to the angels. We can speak the Word to our pets and even to our furniture. When we speak the Word in such a way, we will be the first ones nourished by our speaking. We do not need to spend a long time to enjoy the Lord in the Word early in the morning. Ten to fifteen minutes is sufficient to get nourished and have a good start of a new day. We need to practice this.

WALKING BY AND ACCORDING TO OUR SPIRIT MINGLED WITH THE SPIRIT

We also must learn to walk by and according to our spirit mingled with the Spirit (Gal. 5:16; Rom. 8:4). Praise the Lord that we have a spirit and that our spirit is mingled with the divine Spirit! What a provision! Our God has created us with a spirit and has even regenerated our spirit. Immediately after regenerating us, He stays with us as the Spirit to be one with us and even to mingle Himself with us as one spirit (1 Cor. 6:17). Now we have such a mingled spirit. After having a good start in the morning, we should continue to walk, to live, to do everything by this mingled spirit and with this mingled spirit all day long. We must learn to practice this.

Many married couples cannot avoid having problems with each other. Very few can avoid these problems because the husband and the wife are so close, and they know each other so well. They feel that they do not need to be careful, so there are always chances for them to get into the self or the flesh. These chances are snares and traps to get you. You must learn to walk and to speak, to talk, by the Spirit. Many times, Satan would send your spouse to tempt you. He or she may say a hard word to you or give you a long face. But at that time we have to learn how to walk, how to behave, how to have our being and living by the Spirit. Do not talk to your spouse by yourself. Talk to your spouse with the mingled spirit. This is the way that you can always be ready to speak in the meetings.

LIVING CHRIST FOR HIS MAGNIFICATION
BY THE BOUNTIFUL SUPPLY
OF THE SPIRIT OF JESUS CHRIST

We must live Christ for His magnification by the bountiful supply of the Spirit of Jesus Christ, and this bountiful supply is right within us (Phil. 1:19-21; Gal. 2:20). The Lord has given us a wonderful provision. First, we have His Word in our hand. Second, we have the Holy Spirit, who is the bountiful Spirit of the Lord Jesus Christ, living in us, in our spirit, which has been regenerated and strengthened. We have such a provision, and we can live Christ by this divine provision. If we are such persons, we will surely have something to speak when we come to the meeting.

What kind of Christian do you want to be? Do you want to be a cold, dumb, dormant, dying, lukewarm, defeated, and backsliding one? Or do you want to be a Christian who loves the Lord and who is living, refreshing, and active. Why is Christianity not powerful? It is because most of the Christians in the denominations have been stripped of their riches. They have been annulled and even choked to death. This is why they need a religious service in which one person speaks to them. But in the Lord's recovery it should be different. The Lord desires to recover a meeting with all the members speaking to function. But this depends upon our Christian walk. We must love the

Lord, we must be revived, and we must live a victorious life. We must abide in the fellowship with the Lord daily and hourly, and we must be praying persons. We must enjoy the Lord in the Word early in the morning to have a new start of each day. We must walk and have our being by and according to the mingled spirit, and we must live Christ. If we are such persons day after day and throughout each day, we will be ready to speak in the meetings. Something of Christ will always be bubbling out of us. The Spirit will become a flow out from our innermost being to flow out all the riches of Christ by the Spirit (John 7:37-39).

CHAPTER FOUR

THE SPEAKING IN OUR MEETINGS

(4)

Scripture Reading: Acts 5:42; 8:4; 2 Tim. 4:2; 1 John 1:9; Acts 13:52; Eph. 5:18; Acts 4:31, 8; 13:9; Phil. 3:8-10, 12-14; Col. 3:16; John 15:7; 1 John 2:14; Eph. 5:19; 1 Cor. 14:26, 4-5, 12, 31

In order to enrich and enliven our meeting, we must learn how to speak the word of the Lord in the Scriptures. We must learn to speak and not just read the word. We must also learn to have a corporate speaking of the word in our meetings. This practice is new among the Lord's children. Everyone in the meeting should exercise his spirit and pay much attention to speaking and listening. When one speaks, the others should listen. When we have the speaking that utters and releases the holy word, the riches of God's word will be prevailing to touch all the attendants. We must practice this.

In order to be a speaking one in our meetings, we should be people with a proper character. Without a proper living, our speaking will have no backing. Our daily living, our character, or what we are, is the real backing of our speaking. In the previous chapter we saw eight points concerning the kind of persons we need to be so that we can be the proper speaking ones. In this chapter we want to see nine more aspects.

SPEAKING CHRIST TO ALL KINDS OF PEOPLE DAILY IN SEASON AND OUT OF SEASON

We need to be those who speak Christ to all kinds of people daily in season and out of season (Acts 5:42; 8:4; 2 Tim. 4:2). We should speak Christ to people from every tribe, tongue, people, and nation (Rev. 5:9). In Mark 16:15 the Lord Jesus charged us to preach the gospel to all the creation. This indicates that we should pick up the burden for the preaching of the gospel to such an extent that we would speak to whatever is around us. We should speak to the mountains, the trees, the rivers, the animals, and the entire creation. If we practice this, we will become exercised in speaking. This will strengthen us to speak with power. If we speak awkwardly, that will weaken our speaking and even weaken the contents of our speaking. This is why we should practice speaking Christ all the time even though no person may be present. We always have the entire creation to speak to. I am grateful to the Lord that I practiced this when I was a young man.

When I talk to the saints about the matter of speaking, some tell me that it is not the right time for them to speak. According to their realization, no time is the right time for us to speak. But we have much time to talk on the telephone. It seems that every hour is available for gossip, but no time is available for speaking Christ. This is why Paul charged Timothy to speak the word of God in season and out of season (2 Tim. 4:2). Whether the time is the right time or the "wrong time" for us to speak, we still have to speak. In season or out of season, we have to speak. Our obligation is to speak forth Christ. To speak Christ is never wrong.

When we gossip or speak foolishly, we make ourselves useless. Nothing can destroy our speaking of Christ like a telephone call. To gossip on the telephone is a real temptation. The telephone is a part of American life, but we should not be addicted to talking on it. Sometimes the telephone can be like fly paper. Once we get stuck to it, we cannot get away. The more we indulge in vain talk on the telephone, the more we kill our spirit. Sometimes after talking on the telephone, we are unable to pray because our loose talk has deadened us. Why would we not talk to people about the Lord and about the holy Word? We should learn to save our time and even our spirit by escaping from unnecessary talk on the telephone.

DEALING WITH SINS THOROUGHLY

We also must be ones who deal with our sins thoroughly

(1 John 1:9). We must be sin dealing people. We should not tolerate sin in any way. During the day our hands get dirty, and they pick up many germs spontaneously, so we have to wash them many times. If we washed our hands many times throughout the day, we would be kept from many sicknesses. In like manner, we pick up the germs of sins, of trespasses, throughout the day, so we have to learn to wash ourselves by confessing all of our faults, short-comings, wrongdoings, and trespasses. Many times we overstep our limit. A runner in a race must keep himself within the two white lines of his lane. Otherwise, he will be disqualified. We are a trespassing people. It is so easy for us to overstep in matters, to trespass. A certain punishment in the Old Testament was not to exceed forty stripes (Deut. 25:3). It was quite possible for the person who was exacting the punishment to make an error in counting the number of stripes and overstep the limit by giving forty-one stripes. When exacting such a punishment, it was a safeguard to limit it to thirty-nine stripes, or forty stripes less one (2 Cor. 11:24). It is easy for us to overstep the limit in many matters. When we are laughing about something, we should not laugh too much. If we laugh too much, we are overstepping. When we come back to contact the Lord, our conscience will condemn us for this. If we talk too much on the telephone, this is a trespass for which we need Christ as the trespass offering. We need Christ as our trespass offering all the time.

Before cleaning a room, we may not realize how dirty it is. The more thoroughly that we clean it, the more dirt we will find. We must allow the Lord to search us and cleanse us thoroughly. We must deal with our sins and faults, making a thorough confession to the Lord in His light. When we confess our sins, the Lord forgives us and His blood cleanses us continually (1 John 1:7, 9). The tense of the verb "cleanses" in Greek in 1 John 1:7 is present and continuous. This indicates that the blood of Jesus the Son of God cleanses us all the time, continuously and con-stantly. The blood of Jesus is always ready for us to apply and it cleanses us all day long. Our confessing should be a

daily and hourly matter. As we continually confess our sins,
His blood continually cleanses us.

In 1935 a small number of us stayed with Brother Nee
while he expounded the Song of Songs. During that time I
was dealing with my mistakes, wrongdoings, and trespasses to the uttermost. A certain co-worker and I were
assigned to stay together. Because of our limited facilities,
we had to bring water in a basin from another place to our
rooms so that we could wash ourselves. When I walked past
this brother's bed, some drops of water from the basin I was
carrying frequently fell on it. Then I had to go to him to
confess and ask for forgiveness. For the first few days, he
was not that disturbed by my mistakes. But later when I
apologized to him again, he said, "The worst thing is to sin
and not confess. The best is to not sin. To make mistakes
and apologize is in between the worst and the best." I was
disappointed when the brother said this to me. I told the
Lord, "Lord, I can never be the best. At the most I can only
be in the middle. I can only make mistakes and confess."

If I had been careless, I could have spilled a little water
on the brother's bed without being bothered. But that kind
of careless living or behavior kills our fellowship with the
Lord. Then it is hard for us to pray a prevailing prayer.
The prevailing prayer comes from our constant fellowship
with the Lord, and our constant fellowship with the Lord
depends upon our dealing with our sins. First John 1 tells
us that "God is light" (v. 5). As long as we are in fellowship
with Him, we are in fellowship with the light and are in
the light. When we are in the light, our real situation gets
exposed, and we see all of our failures. We have to confess
them one by one to the Lord, asking forgiveness for item
after item. Then we can have a thorough fellowship with
the Lord, and we are qualified and ready to pray in a
prevailing way.

We must have such a clearance within us if we are
going to speak in the meetings or even if we are going to
speak the gospel to anyone. Otherwise, our speaking will
not be adequate or prevailing. When we do not have a
clearance within our conscience in our fellowship with the

Lord, our speaking will be reluctant. We will not have the full boldness because our conscience has been polluted. This kind of conscience is what the New Testament calls a conscience of offense. Paul said, "I...exercise myself, to have always a conscience without offense toward God and men" (Acts 24:16). We must keep our conscience from all kinds of offenses until we have a conscience without offense. A conscience without offense is a conscience of clearance. When we have such a conscience, we can speak not only to the Lord but also to the unbelieving sinners with boldness. We should not think that we do not need a cleared conscience to speak to sinners. Regardless of whom we speak to, as long as we are speaking the word of God, Christ, or the gospel, we need a cleared conscience. In order for us to learn to speak in the meetings, we must get ourselves cleared up and preserved in a clear condition. We must deal with our sins thoroughly.

BEING FILLED WITH THE SPIRIT INWARDLY

Furthermore, we need to be filled with the Spirit inwardly (Acts 13:52; Eph. 5:18). We need the essential filling of the essential aspect of the Spirit. The Spirit in its essential aspect, the Spirit of essence, the Spirit of life, is for our being, our life, our living, our existence. We have to be filled essentially in our inward being with such a Spirit.

BEING FILLED WITH THE SPIRIT OUTWARDLY

To be filled with the Spirit outwardly is the economical aspect of the Spirit (Acts 4:31, 8; 13:9). It is the economical filling of the economical Spirit. We must have the Spirit of power economically for our work, for our doing, for our moving. We all need to be filled with the Spirit in His two aspects—we need to be filled inwardly so that we are full of life and filled outwardly so that we are full of power and authority.

When I was young, I was taught that the inward and outward aspects of the Spirit were miraculous things that were hard to obtain. One had to fast, pray, deal with many things, and wait on the Lord. But over the years, I found out from the Word and from my experience that the inward and outward filling of the Spirit are miraculous yet normal. D. L. Moody said that regeneration was the greatest miracle. What a miracle it is that a dirty, vile sinner could become a son of God! Yet the experience of regeneration is very normal and transpires in a moment of time. As long as a person opens his heart to the Lord in prayer, believing into Him and calling upon His name, he gets regenerated. This is so normal, but it transpires by the Holy Spirit in our spirit; in this sense it is altogether miraculous. Romans 10:8 indicates that this filling Spirit as the word is even in our mouth and in our heart. When we open up our mouth to call on the name of the Lord and confess all of our sins to Him, we are filled within spontaneously and normally. We then need to exercise our faith that we have been filled with the Spirit both inwardly and outwardly. To exercise our faith is to set our being upon the word of God. We say "amen" to what God says in the Bible—this is faith. Both the inward and outward filling of the Spirit are normal and easy for us to experience.

To be a speaking one, we need the inward filling. Then we have the content. We also need the outward filling. Then we have the power and the authority. We may have a burden to speak, yet it may be hard for us to speak because we are short of the infilling of the Spirit. The infilling is short because our dealing with the Lord is not thorough. We do not empty ourselves of things other than the Lord Himself to allow Him to fill us to the brim. Also, if we do not have a proper dealing with the Lord, we will not be fully released to have the strong faith that we are clothed with the Spirit as our authority. Then our speaking will not be powerful. Instead it may be vain talk. When we deal with the Lord properly and adequately, we will have the assurance, the faith, that the Spirit of power is upon us. We believe this because the Bible tells us so. Then when we speak, our speaking will be powerful and prevailing. We all need to practice this.

When we speak anything concerning Christ, we have to

speak in a way in which we are exercising our spirit and even our whole being to believe the Word of God. We should not speak anything concerning the Lord in a light way. When we speak in the meetings, our speaking should be full of the exercise of the spirit. Our entire being must also be exercised. I saw certain saints speaking in the meetings with little, if any, exercise of the spirit. It seemed as if they needed to lie down to get some rest. We need to learn to speak in the same way that we speak when we lose our temper. Whenever we speak in our temper, we speak by exercising our spirit. Our spirit is strong when we lose our temper. Without the exercise and release of the spirit, no one can lose their temper. This, of course, is the release of the spirit in a negative way. When we speak in the meetings, however, we must learn in the same principle to release our spirit in a positive way.

ACCUMULATING THE EXPERIENCES OF CHRIST

In order to be the speaking ones in our meetings, we must also accumulate the experiences of Christ. From Philippians 3:8-10 and 12-14, we can see that Paul was accumulating the experiences of Christ day after day. Paul was pursuing Christ. The Greek word for *pursue* in Philippians 3 is *dioko*, which is also the word for *persecute*. Before he was saved, Paul persecuted Christ. After being saved, Paul continued to persecute Christ in a positive sense. He would not let the Lord go; he pursued Christ to the uttermost. Because he sought after Christ in such a way, he accumulated the experiences of Christ continually. All day long Paul was enjoying the addition of these experiences. This is why Paul had so much to say about Christ. Many times when we come to the meetings, we do not have much experience of Christ as a base, or a foundation, for our speaking. We are short of experiences. We can speak the word, but our speaking of the word needs a backing, and this backing is our real experience of Christ.

KEEPING A RICH STORAGE OF THE LORD'S WORD

We also must keep a rich storage of the Lord's word

(Col. 3:16; John 15:7; 1 John 2:14). If we would just practice to pray-read two to four verses from the Word every morning, and we do this week after week and month after month, we will gain a rich storage of the living word. The word will not just be in our memory but it will be something stored within us. Many riches of the word of God and of Christ will be stored richly within us. The riches of Christ are embodied in the holy Word. This is what makes the Bible different from all the other books. I have been reading the Bible for many years, but the more I read it, the more riches I receive. We have the same experience whenever we read the publications of the ministry that expound the Bible in the way of life. The more that we abide in the word, the more light we receive.

We need to dwell upon the word every day. The best time is in the morning, and the best way is to pick up two to four verses from a specific book of the New Testament. Do not pick up two verses in the morning in a random way. Do not choose the verses that fit your taste. Instead pick a book of the New Testament and pray-read your way through it, verse by verse. If you want to start with Philippians, you can begin with verses 1 and 2 of the first chapter: "Paul and Timothy, slaves of Christ Jesus, to all the saints in Christ Jesus who are in Philippi, with the overseers and deacons: Grace to you and peace from God our Father and the Lord Jesus Christ." The first word of verse 1, "Paul," is very rich. We can pray, "Lord Jesus— Paul! I want to be a Paul today." Then we can go on to speak, "Paul and Timothy." "O Lord, not only Paul but also Timothy. Hallelujah! Paul and Timothy! Thank You for the Paul's in the church life today and the younger Timothy's." Every single word of the Bible is good. We can read it, pray it, and speak it to the Lord and to ourselves. How rich the phrases "slaves of Christ Jesus" and "to all the saints" are! Every word in the Bible is so meaningful. When we come back to these verses in Philippians again with an open and empty spirit, we will receive more light. We may say, "Lord, thank You that this is Paul and not Saul. It is not the natural Saul but the regenerated Paul."

Every time we come to the Word in a proper way, we will receive some fresh points from the Lord.

When we exercise our spirit to read the Bible, the Spirit within our spirit reacts and echos with something. The Spirit of God explores the depths of God concerning Christ and shows them to us in our spirit for our realization and participation (1 Cor. 2:10). In this way, verse after verse and phrase after phrase from the Bible can be stored within us, and we can keep a rich storage of the Lord's word. When we come to any meeting or meet with anyone, it will be easy for us to speak, and we will have the material to release because we have the experiences of Christ and the riches of the holy word accumulated and stored within us. This will strengthen and enrich our speaking and even encourage us to speak.

KNOWING SOME OF THE HYMNS ON CHRIST, THE SPIRIT, THE CHURCH, LIFE, ETC. IN OUR HYMNAL

The speaking ones in our meetings must know some of the hymns on Christ, the Spirit, the church, life, etc. in our hymnal (1 Cor. 14:26; Eph. 5:19; Col. 3:16). If we want to know the hymnal, we must spend some time to get into the table of contents of our hymnal. The hymns are divided into thirty major categories arranged in a proper sequence according to the truth. Each major category has a number of subcategories. Under the major category "Experience of Christ" there are thirty-two subcategories. Thank the Lord that we have the Bible and also a hymnal with hymns that were composed according to the truths of the Bible. Our main hymnal has one thousand and eighty hymns, and our supplement has two hundred and sixty-eight hymns. We composed our main hymnal with so many to show others that we in the Lord's recovery have the knowledge of the truth. We put many hymns into the hymnal mainly for our knowledge of the truth and not for our singing. Among these one thousand and eighty hymns, there are at least over three hundred very good hymns which are good for singing and for speaking. We should know a hymn like #499—"Oh, what a life! Oh, what a peace!"—and we should learn to speak it. From now on we have to learn to use the hymns firstly for speaking. Singing the hymns is not as important as speaking them. We have discovered in the Word and in our experience that speaking a hymn is much more important and profitable than singing it. Hymn #501—"O glorious Christ, Savior mine"—and hymn #539—"O Lord, Thou art the Spirit!"—are other excellent hymns that we should know and learn to speak. We must endeavor to learn a number of the crucial hymns in our hymnal.

DESPERATELY ENDEAVORING TO BUILD UP A HABIT OF SPEAKING IN ANY MEETING

We all have to desperately endeavor to build up a habit of speaking in any meeting (1 Cor. 14:26, 4-5, 12, 31). We must be desperate to build up a habit to speak. This habit has to be built up universally in the Lord's recovery. We do not have such a habit due to the background of Christianity, and our function has been killed because of this background. Many Chinese people do not speak English well because they did not have the habit of speaking English when they grew up, and they still do not have this habit. I did not pick up the habit of speaking English until I began to minister the word in the United States in 1962. It was hard for me to acquire this habit, but for my grandchildren it was easy because they grew up in an English-speaking environment. If we learn to build up a habit of speaking in any meeting, our children, the new ones, will spontaneously become speaking ones. The new ones will follow the trend and the atmosphere in the meeting. They will pick up the habit of speaking easily. We must endeavor to do this because it is not just for ourselves but for the benefit of the Lord's recovery.

We have to overthrow the old, traditional, and unscriptural way of meeting. Brother Nee told us that the Lord's Day message meeting with one person speaking and the others listening was a waste, that it was not worthwhile to maintain, and that it was according to the customs of the nations (see *Church Affairs*, pp. 68-75, 85-86). Although we have to overthrow this practice, it is hard to overthrow because it is our habit. If we give up this habit and do not have anything to replace it, we will have nothing. It seems that we cannot live or survive as a Christian without this traditional way of meeting. This is why we need a new start in the recovery, and this new start depends on us. If we would pick up the burden to practice this fellowship in order to be the speaking ones in our meetings, a habit will be built up among us. How could anyone take away the speaking of English from the people of the United States? It is impossible because this has been founded and built up as a habit among them. We also need such a foundation of speaking Christ in all our meetings. If not within five years, perhaps within ten years, such a habit will be prevailing among us. Then even the unbelievers will have their concept changed concerning the Christian meeting. Most of the unbelievers today have the concept that a Christian meeting is to have a pastor or a preacher speak while all the others listen to him. Even before they get saved, they already have this concept. We have to overthrow this practice and build up another habit.

All of us can speak. We have the Bible, a hymnal, the Life-study Messages, and other spiritual publications to speak. If we spoke a Life-study Message together, this would make the best message full of the divine riches and the refreshing utterances. We should not merely read the message but speak it, and this speaking should not be an individual speaking but a corporate speaking. May we all rise up to pick up the burden to be the speaking ones in our meetings. May we be desperate to practice speaking and to build up a habit of speaking. This is a great thing for the Lord's recovery, for His move on this earth, and this practice will really build up every saint in life.

ALWAYS HAVING SOMETHING TO SPEAK IN ALL THE MEETINGS AS A FREEWILL OFFERING TO GOD AND TO THE AUDIENCE

We should always have something to speak in all the meetings as a freewill offering to God and to the audience

(1 Cor. 14:26 and note 1). In all our meetings we should not speak merely out of being forced or compelled to speak. Our speaking should be an offering of our free will to God for His glory and satisfaction and to the attendants for their enlightening, nourishing, and building up.

THE SPEAKING IN OUR MEETINGS

(5)

Scripture Reading: 1 Cor. 14:26; Heb. 10:25; 1 Cor. 14:40

BREAKING ALL FORMALITIES
AND AVOIDING ANY KIND OF PROGRAM

In this chapter, we want to see something particular concerning the nature of our meetings. In our meetings we should break all formalities and avoid any kind of program. First Corinthians 14:26 and Hebrews 10:25 are "show windows" to show us what the meetings were like in the ancient times when the apostles were still on this earth. Through these show windows, we can see what was happening at that time. Meetings were going on, yet without formalities or programs.

First Corinthians 14:26 says, "What is it then, brothers? Whenever you come together, each one has a psalm, has a teaching, has a revelation, has a tongue, has an interpretation. Let all things be done for building up." According to this verse, formalities are not needed in the Christian meetings. In Paul's time there were no formalities and no programs in the meetings. When the church comes together, "each one has." Until each one in the meeting presents what he has, no one knows what subject or subjects the meeting will cover or the order in which things will be presented. Surely in such a meeting there can be no regulation, program, or formality. We have to break all the formalities today and avoid any kind of program.

Hebrews 10:25 says, "Not forsaking the assembling of ourselves together, as the custom with some is, but exhorting one another, and so much the more as you see the day drawing near." This verse indicates that programs are not necessary for the Christian meetings. In the

Christian meeting, we all have to exhort one another.
Surely this kind of meeting is without formality or any
kind of program. Our meetings today should be like those
in the ancient times.

In the four Gospels, the Lord Jesus had many meetings
in His ministry, yet with no formality and no program.
Verse four of hymn #1281 in *Hymns* says, "In the
meetings, in the meetings, On the mountain, at the shore."
This is a description of the way the Lord Jesus held His
meetings. Sometimes He held His meetings on the mountain
top, and quite often He held meetings on the seashore,
mostly around the Sea of Galilee. We have published a
book entitled *How to Meet* from messages given in the
spring of 1969 and 1970. The light concerning many
principles of meeting came to us from 1966 to 1972. Hymn
#1281 was written according to that light, but in our
practice after 1972, it seems that much of this light
disappeared from among us. However, in our practice of
the church life at this time, the light is returning.

WELL-SPEAKING IN THE MEETINGS

Today's Christianity has fallen into a religion. A
religion is composed of organization, hierarchy, formalities,
and programs. In religion there is no Christ, no incarnation
of the Triune God, no grace, and no reality. Rather, it is
full of hierarchy with programs and formalities. As a
church, whenever we come together we must be full of
Christ and the incarnation of the Triune God. Then we will
be filled with grace and reality, and all the grace and
reality will be released by our speaking.

The speaking of Christ by the attendants of the
meetings is well-speaking. The word "blessing" in Greek
simply means "well-speaking." Ephesians 1:3-14 is Paul's
blessing to God, and that blessing is nothing other than a
well-speaking. When we come together we must speak well
about our Triune God, about the Father, about the Son,
and about the Spirit. Our well-speaking is our blessing.

To speak blessing is not merely to speak the word
"blessing." One hymn begins, "Blessing and honor and

glory be Thine" (*Hymns*, #241). I like this short song, but I doubt that those who sing it know what the blessing is. They may only know how to sing the word "blessing." I hope that some would compose a song of blessing from Ephesians 1:3-14. We need such a portion as these verses to be the real contents of our blessing. The contents of this blessing would be the well-speaking concerning our Triune God and how He has blessed us with the eternal economy of the Father, the Son, and the Holy Spirit—with the Father's selection and predestination, the Son's redemption, and the Spirit's sealing and pledging. The blessing is simply the well-speaking.

When we give a testimony concerning the Lord Jesus or our experience of Him, our testimony is a blessing. When a brother gives a testimony that he has enjoyed Christ as the One who can overcome his bad temper, his testimony is a blessing to the Triune God. It is hard for a young man to overcome his temper, and it is hard for a young woman to overcome her murmuring. Philippians 2:14 says, "Do all things without murmurings and reasonings." Murmurings are of our emotion, mostly by the sisters; reasonings are of our mind, mostly by the brothers. How can we overcome our temper, murmurings, and reasonings? These are small things, but these "gophers" are hard for us to overcome. It is very difficult for any descendant of Adam to overcome his temper. Quite often we do not know when our temper will come. Perhaps you will have a good time with the Lord with two verses, but after five minutes the "gopher" of temper will come for no apparent reason, and you will feel unhappy with your wife. The temper is the worst "gopher."

In a meeting I could give a testimony of how I have enjoyed Christ as the temper-overcoming One. I may say, "Fifty or sixty years ago, I was a strong man with a quick temper, but one day I found the secret of enjoying Christ. Because of the enjoyment of Christ, it is not easy for the gopher to come to me. The guard that keeps the gopher away is the all-inclusive, compound, life-giving Spirit who is the consummation of the processed Triune God. Every time that I call on His name, He is so real. He is not only my guard but also my safeguard. I have experienced Him much in this way." A testimony given along this line is a blessing to the Triune God. It is a well-speaking of the all-inclusive, compound, processed, consummated, life-giving, indwelling, sevenfold intensified Spirit. This kind of testifying is a well-speaking concerning our Christ; therefore, this is our blessing to Him.

There should always be this kind of blessing in the church meetings. In the big meetings and the small meetings the saints should come together all the time to bless our Triune God, not just to sing "Blessing and honor and glory be Thine." Each one should open his mouth to speak something concerning the divine Trinity, something concerning our Father, concerning the Son, and concerning this all-inclusive, compound, consummated, processed, all-inclusive Spirit. We cannot exhaust such speaking.

We do have help for our speaking. We have the Bible, a hymnal, and many other publications in life. We can bring any of these publications, such as the *Truth Lessons* or the Life-study Messages, and speak them to one another. If we speak the printed pages of these books, what a rich meeting that will be! It will be full of the light of the truth and full of the nourishment of life. What takes place in that meeting will be a long blessing out of our mouth to our Father, to His Son, and to His wonderful Spirit. This is what the Christian meeting should be. However in today's religion there is hierarchy, clergy, laity, programs, and formality. This is why we must have a turn.

ALL FUNCTIONING IN A DECENT ORDER

Formalities eliminate the liberty for the attendants to function, thus annulling their functioning organ. Many of us have attended the meetings in the denominations. Our functioning organ was annulled there, and we ourselves were nearly deadened to the uttermost. This is because these meetings were filled with formalities and programs. Programs limit the function to certain attendants, thus robbing the other attendants of their opportunity to function. All the regular meetings of the church should be kept open and free for all the attendants to have an equal chance to function. We must maintain this atmosphere in our meetings until the time of our rapture.

A special gathering for a certain purpose is different from a regular church meeting. In the New Testament, there are some special meetings, some special gatherings. Perhaps the church has to carry out a particular matter. The elders can call a special gathering to speak to the saints about this matter. Furthermore, if some of the saints have a burden to release a word of revelation or a word of vision, a special gathering will be needed.

Every function in the regular meeting of the church, regardless of what kind, should be in a decent order (1 Cor. 14:40). There is no program and no form, but the functions should be in a decent order in a very becoming way. In this matter, do not make an offense and do not play. First Corinthians 10:7 says, "Neither become idolaters, as some of them; as it is written, The people sat down to eat and drink, and stood up to play." To play means to have entertainment. Whatever we do in the meetings should be for the genuine worship of God, not for fun. In the past we have had some wonderful meetings, but some of the attendants were not well-speaking but were playing in their speaking. This is wrong. You have to release your spirit, but you must be decent. You must do all things in the meeting in a decent order.

CHAPTER SIX

CONCERNING VISITING PEOPLE FOR GOSPEL PREACHING AND HOME MEETINGS FOR RAISING THE NEW BELIEVERS

In this chapter we would like to fellowship concerning visiting people for gospel preaching and having home meetings for raising the new believers. We have been studying these matters for over three and a half years. We have learned much and have picked up many good points related to these practices.

We practiced visiting people for gospel preaching for nearly one and a half years in Taipei. Within the three terms of our training there, about twenty-six thousand people were baptized, mostly through the trainees. Through our practice there, we have learned much and have discovered many secrets. What we have learned will help you to save your time and to be saved from many troubles.

In Taipei we first endeavored to determine whether visiting people by door-knocking would really be workable. We found out that visiting people for the preaching of the gospel really works. We also found out that door-knocking can be done quickly but that we do not need to go too fast. We were too quick in our door-knocking. In a good sense, we realized that we should not have had that many baptisms. Eventually, thirty-eight thousand people have been baptized in Taipei, but our manpower can only take care of about six thousand. To take care of six thousand people as newborn babes needs manpower. Without the manpower, it cannot be done. About thirty thousand baptized ones have been left without much care. This became a burden to the feeling of the serving ones and to the entire church. Those thirty thousand confessed the name of the Lord, they called on this holy name, and they were baptized, but there has not been the adequate care for them. This was not pleasing and encouraging to us. Therefore, we have made a strong decision that from this term of the training we will instruct the trainees and the local saints that knocking on doors to get people saved and baptized and setting up home meetings to take care of them should be done in a proper proportion. We will proportion our time for these two things. We should not spend ninety-five percent of our time on door-knocking and baptisms and only five percent of our time and manpower to take care of the new ones. This is not wise. From now on we should not go too fast, caring only for the number of baptisms.

What we are fellowshipping here is a result of our study. This is not a law or a constitution for the Lord's new move. We do not have anything constitutional, but we have a living spirit within us. Whatever we practice should be very flexible. In the past three and a half years, we have shifted our practice one way and then the other. We have shifted our way in the training more than five or six times. We have to do it this way. Students of science must change their way in the laboratory many times in order to discover principles and rules. Through our practice we have learned something. But after one week our practice may change again. The coach of a basketball team will change his ways quite often. He will be very flexible, not caring for his instruction but for getting the ball into the basket. He only cares for how many goals his team gets.

What we are doing now, we have never done before. We did much preaching forty years ago, but we never practiced the present way. The present way was quite new to me, and it is still new to me because we have not picked up the adequate experiences. Only experience will teach us things in a practical way. To talk is one thing, but to practice is another. Your talking with many opinions is not needed if you have not lifted your finger for this work. We must put not only our finger but also our entire being into this. This is what we did in Taipei.

Before we began to practice the new way, we had no assurance that we could gain people through preaching the gospel by visiting them in their homes. We did not know how many we would get. The year after I left mainland China, I went to the Philippines and began to charge the saints in the local churches to bring at least one sinner to the Lord each year. All the attendants in the meetings felt that this would be easy. Everyone said that they could gain one person in three hundred and sixty-five days. Every year for eleven years I stayed in the Philippines for three or four months. In not one of those years did they make their goal. It was altogether a failure. Among the hundreds of saints who did love the Lord, not more than ten made the goal. Afterwards, they had no assurance or confidence that this could be worked out.

However, since we have picked up the new way and practiced it, we have the scientific assurance. I can assure you that as long as you knock on doors to preach the gospel in a proper way, you will gain one person for every twenty doors that you knock on. If out of twenty doors there is not one son of peace (Luke 10:5-6), something is wrong. It is easy to knock on twenty doors in one and a half hours.

THE COMPOSITION OF THE GOSPEL TEAMS

As a rule, each gospel team that goes out should be composed of three persons of different ages, a young one, an old one, and one in the middle. Ideally the youngest should be a sister, the middle one a brother, and the third one an older brother or sister. The older one is for the opening of the doors. If a team of three young men goes out, almost no doors will be opened to them. People may be afraid of them and not dare to open their doors. However, if an older brother or sister would go with them, many doors will be open. Many doors are open especially to an older sister. We have found out that the older sisters are very valuable in visiting people with the gospel.

At the beginning of our training, we knew this in principle. We arranged for every team to have an older one.

Eventually we discovered that the older ones are welcomed everywhere. The older one should knock on the door while the younger ones stand back. Once inside a house, it is best if the young sister speaks. We have found on many occasions that the most prevailing ones to bring people into the faith were the young sisters. The brothers are mostly good for putting people into the water of baptism. When the young or middle-aged brother would go to baptize people, either the young sister or the older brother or sister should help to prepare the water.

PRACTICAL INSTRUCTIONS FOR VISITING PEOPLE

There are a few instructions we should follow in door-knocking. First, at each door knock three times not using more than half a minute. If the door does not open, immediately turn to the next door. Do not waste time. Then when a door is opened to you and you enter and begin to speak, learn to sense whether there is the possibility that this person will get baptized that day. You may sense that there is no possibility on that day, although he might be a son of peace two weeks later. Perhaps you will find out that he just quarreled with his wife. While you were knocking, they were still quarreling. When you entered, you entered into a fighting situation. How could this person be a son of peace this day? Even if he was chosen, this may not be the time for him to be called. Do not foolishly waste your time. After five minutes at the most, you could realize that was the wrong time to talk to him. You should not stay, but nicely tell him that you will come to visit another time.

Perhaps you may find a Christian who has been in the faith for ten years, attending a denomination. This one may be very talkative and tell you that he loves the truth, admires your practice of visiting people, and many other things. When you hear this, simply greet the brother and leave. Usually, you will gain nothing by talking with such a person; you will waste your time.

Perhaps you will have knocked on nineteen doors without gaining one person. Quite often nothing happens up to the last door. One hour and ten minutes might have been used, with less than a half hour of your time left. Do not give up. Try two or three more doors. Quite often the Lord would test us. Up to the last door there may only be ten minutes left, but when you get into this door, everything is in the heavens. Here is a son of peace, and the rest is easy. I have often heard this kind of testimony. One sister suffered six nights without getting one person. She prayed and fasted, and eventually the seventh night her team baptized about six people. In the first home there were three baptisms.

BEARING FRUIT FOR A ONEFOLD INCREASE YEARLY

In every team that goes out for the gospel, there should be at least one local saint. Saints from other localities or full-timers may be gone the following week, and the new babes would be left as orphans. We must be clear that when we knock on doors, we local saints are the nursing mothers of the new ones whom we bring to the Lord. After going out to knock on doors, we will have new babes to take care of. Whoever is gained will be our child.

We can visit people about two weekends every three months to get about two new believers. Every three months, we should go out to knock on doors. We do not need to go out every week. In the first three months we will have one or two new ones to take care of. Then in the next three months, we will bring in another one or two. We will then have three or four under our care. In each three-month period, we will gain one or two new ones. In this way, the saints will preach the gospel by visiting people throughout the year. Each one will have some babes under his care.

Suppose that everyone who means business with the Lord for His recovery would preach the gospel in this way. This would be wonderful. At least one fourth of the church would do it, so out of one hundred meeting together, twenty-five will go out. Each of these twenty-five will gain about four persons, or about one every three months. I believe each one will get more than four, but there will be four that remain. You may get seven or nine, but at the end of the year four will still remain. Do not forget the Lord's word in John 15:16: "I appointed you that you should go forth and bear fruit, and that your fruit should remain." To go forth is to visit people; to have remaining fruit is through the home meetings. I have found through the years that the most confident way to gain people is by knocking on their doors and that the most certain way to keep those that we gain is through the home meetings. To go out to knock on people's doors is the scientific way to get the increase, and to have the home meetings is the scientific way to have remaining fruit. Twenty-five out of one hundred saints, each bringing in four persons, will yield a one hundred percent increase, a onefold increase.

In Manila when I proposed to the saints to bring one sinner to the Lord yearly, I did not have the assurance that they could do it. However, I have the assurance this can be done in the new way. It depends upon your doing. I do not expect that all the saints meeting in a local church will go out for the gospel. This is not possible. Some might not be so strong, some might be sick, and some might be otherwise occupied. However, in general, twenty-five percent of our manpower can gain a onefold yearly increase for the church.

This way is not too hard. Every team that goes out for the gospel will get one person if they do it properly. Within two and a half hours you can knock on thirty doors. You have to manage your time. Do not stay in a home more than five minutes unless you find a son of peace. This son of peace is worth staying with for one hour. Your staying with him will lay a good foundation and will open the entire home for further visits.

THE FIRST HOME MEETING

After baptizing a new one, immediately have the first home meeting with him for one hour, teaching him the Lord as the life-giving Spirit indwelling his regenerated spirit and leading him to pray by calling on the name of the Lord. You should stay there for at least one hour; the longer you can stay with him, the better. Do not be greedy for numbers. You have one person already and you should be satisfied. You have one treasure; do not let it go. Stay with this person to give him his first lesson, taking as much time as the situation allows.

The first lesson is to tell this new one that the very Savior in whom he has believed and whom he has received, Jesus Christ, today is the life-giving Spirit (1 Cor. 15:45b). Do not consider this as a deeper teaching. This is not a deeper teaching. Charge him to learn the "alphabet." Of the ABCs, this is A. Do not be afraid to spend too much time. The longer the time is, the better. Tell him that the Lord Jesus today is the life-giving Spirit. As the Spirit, He is just like the air. He is everywhere; He is omnipresent. Tell him that the Lord as the Spirit is now within him. Then tell him that he also has a human spirit and that this is the right organ for him to contact God. Most people do not know that each human being has a spirit as a particular organ for him to contact God. Illustrate to him that, if he did not have two eyes, he could not realize color, and that if he did not have two ears, he could not realize sound. If he does not exercise his spirit, there will be no way for him to realize that God is Spirit. Tell him that the Lord Jesus today is the life-giving Spirit, that he has a spirit, and that this divine Spirit abides in his spirit.

After this, tell him that to pray is simply to call on the Lord Jesus who is now the Spirit within him. Then lead him to pray by calling on His name. Tell him that from that day he is a person who has Christ the Lord within him. He is not a non-Christian who does not have the Lord Jesus within him. Rather, the Lord Jesus is in him. Bring him into such knowledge and lead him to pray. Tell him that in any problem he might face he should call on the Lord and pray. This must be included in the first lesson.

When you speak with a new one on each point, you have to open a proper verse to him. Concerning the Lord being the life-giving Spirit you must open to 1 Corinthians 15:45b, point it out to him, and help him to read that portion: "The last Adam became a life-giving Spirit." Ask him to read it, once, twice, and a third time. Also, ask him to read loudly, not merely shouting, but as a calling. Lead him to say, "How good, Lord! Now You are a life-giving Spirit!" You may also choose a verse concerning the human spirit. You can use John 4:24: "God is Spirit; and those who worship Him must worship in spirit and reality." Tell him that this spirit is his human spirit. Give him verses in this way, but do not give him too many—at the most three or four. Read these verses and help him to become familiar with them. We must do this one thing immediately. Do not wait until the next day to do it. Even if he would say that he does not have much time, still beg him to do it. Tell him that you want to spend this golden time with him for his sake and his benefit. We have found that this will render much help. Immediately after his baptism, in the first meeting, build up such a practice. This is what will help him to lay a very good foundation. Many times in the past, we gave this first lesson too late.

MEETING WITH THE NEW ONES

Continue to have home meetings with the new ones once every three days for the first month to raise them in the Lord. You need to go back to visit the new ones within not more than three days. In one month's time you should visit them ten times, three days apart. Then after the first month, change to visiting them once a week. Continue to have home meetings with them once a week for two or three months. During these two or three months, you will look into their situation. Different persons will have different situations. According to their situation, you should try to help them realize that Christians should be flocked together. Christians cannot be independent, separate, or far away from other Christians. They need to meet with other Christians. Try your best to bring them into one of the nearby small group meetings. Also try during these two or three months to bring them into the bigger meetings, especially on the Lord's Day. However, in the first month, when you visit them ten times, you do not need to bring them to the small group meetings or the bigger meetings unless they ask about them.

They may ask if you have a church. Do not say that you do not, asking, "What do you mean by the church? Do you mean the church building?" If they ask if you have a church, you should ask them if they would like to go. If they answer yes, then make arrangements to bring them the following Lord's Day. This is just to fit in with their feeling and their need. You have to take care of a new one in this way. Otherwise, you will spoil the entire situation.

We hope that within half a year, everyone will be brought into the regular church meetings. But we still need to go to help them in their home meetings up to the end of one year. Also, we should lead them to practice what we are doing in preaching the gospel and helping the home meetings. After one year, we must have the confidence that they have been brought into the church life and can serve the Lord in the church on their own without our help. At that time we can make it clear to them that they should serve the Lord in the church and do the things that we have been doing. This implies that within that one year, especially in the second half of the year, we must teach them as a coach how to go with us to knock on people's doors for the preaching of the gospel and how to take care of the home meetings. We should instruct them and lead them to do what we are doing, hoping that within one year they will be raised up in the church life.

CARING FOR THE NEW BELIEVERS
WITH DISCERNMENT AND WISDOM

According to our experience in Taipei, the newly baptized believers were of different kinds. Some did not like to read much, while others were very good readers who would receive any kind of book. What you do with them must be based upon your discernment and realization. To visit the home meetings you must exercise with much wisdom. In Colossians 1:28 Paul says, "Whom we announce, warning every man and teaching every man in all wisdom, that we may present every man full-grown in Christ." We need the wisdom. The longer you stay with a new one, the better, but you need to exercise your discernment as to whether that person is one who likes people to stay with him. If you realize that a certain one is this kind of person and he invites you to stay after his baptism to eat with him, do not reject his offer but stay there in faith for dinner. However, in your discernment you may realize that another person would not like to have a guest stay longer than one hour. In that case, do your best to finish within one hour. Do not spoil their taste. Your activity and action should be based upon their disposition and how much they can receive. Do not forget that this may be the first time for them to contact Christians. They do not know much about Christian things, so do not give them a negative, disappointing impression. Rather, in everything you do in your contact with them, give them a very positive impression that would not bother them or spoil them.

This requires our practice. In the use of medicine, doctors take care of the health and condition of their patients. Do not be negligent or careless. You must learn how to discern your patient. We should consider all the new ones as our patients and ourselves as the doctors going to care for them. We must exercise our wisdom to discover the real situation.

What books or other publications you give to the new ones also depends upon their condition, your knowledge, and whether or not you have that book. For this reason you must know the *Life Lessons*, the *Truth Lessons*, the Life-study Messages, and our other books. It is better to go to the new ones with these publications; then when you discover what their need is, perhaps after five minutes of contact, you will have all the right "medicine" with you. You can dispense the right medicine for the right sickness with the proper dosage according to their health.

We also need to be like a teacher in a school who presents things to the students according to their level. A first grade teacher presents mathematics to a certain degree and extent. A second grade teacher gives the pupils something further. When one teaches higher grades, he still teaches mathematics, but his teaching has come up to a higher level. The teaching will be according to the pupils' grade. This way of teaching is needed with the new ones.

Do not say that since you are not "professionals" you cannot do this. We all like to be healthy, so we are learning what to eat. There is much learning to do even in the matter of eating. My wife is learning about healthy food and how to cook, and I am learning of her how to eat. She may cook properly, but if I eat improperly, this will spoil her cooking. Therefore the two of us must match in our learning. This is an illustration of how we must learn to care for others.

TAKING THE NEW WAY FOR THE LORD'S RECOVERY

We should mean business for the Lord's present recovery. In the Lord's recovery there is a need. Christianity has proven that their old way is not workable. The Southern Baptist denomination, which has had annual increases in membership since 1926, recorded a gain of only seven-tenths of a percent from 1986 to 1987. We could not survive if we only had this much increase; we would die out. We need at least thirty percent increase in order to survive to do something for the Lord's recovery. Without new people, what can we do? We have the best teachings and the healthy food, and everything is so excellent, but without new people, we are finished. Look at our situation. It is not dying, but the low rate of increase is bothersome. The old way will not work. How could we trust in the old way? We must change to a new way. We must come back to find the God-ordained way revealed in the holy Word, and we have found this way in the past three and a half years. What we have been speaking in this period of time is altogether biblical and according to God's heart and will.

The first step in this way is to visit people for gospel preaching. Many verses in the Bible tell us that we have to go to people. "How beautiful are the feet of those who announce glad tidings of good things!" (Rom. 10:15). It is a shame that we have been here for years yet have not knocked on so many doors. Many people are living around us. The "fish pond" is right before us, but we have not

fished. Rather, we invite the fish to come to us; this is
ridiculous. We must drop the old way.

All the home meetings should be considered as church
meetings. We must meet in the homes regularly. We must
reconsecrate ourselves for this. In this consecration we
should promise the Lord that every week we will separate
and sanctify at least one evening, preferably two, for the
Lord's move. Every week we should spend two evenings,
two and a half hours each, for the Lord's move. First, we
go out to knock on doors to gain the people; then we
continue to visit them for their home meetings. I have the
assurance that this way is workable. We will gain people
and we will have remaining fruit. We may have a onefold
increase yearly.

DISPENSING THE LORD JESUS THROUGH THE GOSPEL

We must do the gospel work without analyzing, like a
farmer sowing seed. For a farmer to try to determine what
will grow and what will not grow means nothing. He must
simply till the ground, water the plants, and let them grow.
Some will grow very well, while others will not grow well.
In the parable of the sower in Matthew 13, the first sowing
was in vain, the second group of seeds did not have deep
root, and the third group of seeds was choked by the
thorns. Only the last seeds, one-fourth of those sown, grew
well. We do not know which will grow. Experts tell us that
before wheat and tares blossom, no one can tell them
apart. The two look very much alike in stature, color, and
shape until they blossom, the wheat with golden yellow
fruit and the tares with black fruit.

Today we cannot say what will happen. We must
simply do what we should according to the Lord's word. He
says, "Go into all the world and preach the gospel to all the
creation" (Mark 16:15), and we go. He says, "Go therefore
and disciple all the nations" (Matt. 28:19), and we do it. He
says, "He who believes and is baptized shall be saved"
(Mark 16:16), and we do our duty to help people to believe
and be baptized. We do not care who is who. Our goal is
simply to dispense the Lord Jesus through the gospel to all

people. What will come out is not in our hands. It is in His hand. We simply do it.

The earth is full of "fish." Whether you use your time to take care of a hesitating one depends on how much time you have. If one is hesitating, why do you have to spend your time on him? Go to other fish. Some fish are jumping into the boat. Why would you not rather take care of this kind of fish. Do not analyze how to work with the hesitating ones. Let them stay where they are. Farmers do not sow seed into soil when they know that it does not grow anything. There are many people on this earth today. Go to others who are not hesitating.

CHAPTER SEVEN

KNOWING THE HYMNS

Scripture Reading: 1 Cor. 14:26; Eph. 5:18-19; Col. 3:16

If we desire to be the speaking ones in the meetings, we have to know the hymns. In order for us to enrich, strengthen, enliven, refresh, and uplift our meetings, we need to use the hymns. We have seen that according to 1 Corinthians 14:26 and Hebrews 10:25, we need both speaking and singing in our meetings. The speaking is not only the speaking of the word of God or the speaking forth of Christ but also the speaking of the hymns. The first item listed by Paul in 1 Corinthians 14:26 is a psalm. A psalm is poetry. In both Ephesians 5:19 and Colossians 3:16, we are charged to speak in hymns. This indicates that the saints in the early Christian meetings used a lot of hymns. Many times we may not be able to find a verse or some verses in the Bible to meet the real need in the meeting, but we can easily find a hymn to meet the need. This is why we have to know the hymns. If we use the hymns adequately and properly in our meetings, they will be uplifted, enlivened, and refreshed. But we have to do everything in a living way, not in a legal way. Legality brings in death and deadness. We must stay away from the legal deadness. We should try to do everything in a very living way that is flexible and applicable.

OUR WORK WITH THE HYMNS

Brother Nee was the first person to put out a hymnal among us in mainland China. By the time I came into the Lord's recovery in 1932, we had a hymnal of one hundred and eighty-three hymns. The majority of those hymns were translated by Brother Nee. Some new hymns were also written by him and one or two others. That hymnal contained many hymns from the Brethren. Brother Nee entitled that hymnal *The Little Flock*. Many of the missionaries called us "the little flock" fifty or sixty years ago because of the name of our hymnal. Brother Nee announced a few times that "the little flock" was just the title of our hymnal and not a name that we adopted to denominate ourselves. Despite this, people still called us "the little flock." As a result, Brother Nee made the decision to change the name of our hymnal to *Hymns,* which is also the name of our present hymnal.

In the early 1940s we in northern China became prevailing in our gospel work, so I began to collect some hymns for the gospel such as "Rock of Ages" (#1058), "Jesus, lover of my soul" (#1057), and "In tenderness He sought me" (#1068). Because these hymns were so popular, Brother Nee did not collect them in his earlier hymnal. But in the early forties, we felt that we had the need to collect these hymns in a small hymnal for the sake of the gospel work. In 1947 and 1948, many young people in Shanghai were brought into the church life through our work on the campus. At that time our hymnal was not adequate to meet the need of these young people, so I prepared a hymnal with short songs that were good for the young people. Thus, when we moved to Taiwan for the Lord's work, we had three hymnals. The first collection of one hundred and eighty-three hymns was compiled by Brother Nee, and the other two hymnals were compiled by me.

From 1960 to 1961, I was burdened to minister Christ as the life-giving Spirit to the saints in Taiwan. By that time we were short of hymns on Christ, the Spirit, life, and the church. In 1961 I spent two months to write eighty-five new hymns on these subjects. A number of these have been translated and are in our present English hymnal. Hymn #499—"Oh, what a life! Oh, what a peace!"; #501—"O glorious Christ, Savior mine"; and #608—"What mystery, the Father, Son, and Spirit," were written in 1961 in Taipei and translated into English in 1964 in Los Angeles. After I wrote these hymns in Taiwan in 1961, the saints there had four hymnals to bring to the church meetings.

When I came to the United States and the Lord's recovery began in this country in 1962, we had the deep sensation that we needed an adequate hymnal which could greatly help our meetings. When I traveled throughout the United States from 1962 to 1964, I looked at various hymnals to see if there were any hymns that would be useful for our collection. When we compiled the hymns in our hymnal, we also looked into the British Keswick Convention hymnal. Most of those hymns were useful to us, so a number of them were included in our present hymnal. From 1963 to 1964, I wrote about two hundred new hymns which were also included in our hymnal.

Many of the hymns that we collected from other hymnals were adjusted, corrected, and improved by us. Some of the lines were not according to the truth of the Scriptures. Hymn #1068 in our hymnal is a good example of this. I love this hymn very much, so I translated it into Chinese. But it was seriously wrong in one point. The chorus said:

> Oh, the love that sought me!
> Oh, the blood that bought me!
> Oh, the grace that brought me to the fold,
> Wondrous grace that brought me to the fold!

According to the scriptural revelation, the fold signifies the law, or Judaism as the religion of the law, in which God's chosen people were kept and guarded in custody and ward until Christ came (John 10:1-9). The flock, on the other hand, signifies the church as the one Body of Christ (v. 16). At the time this hymn was written, the church was considered as a fold, but the fold in John 10 refers to the Jewish religion. The Lord's desire was to bring the Gentile and the Jewish believers together into one flock to form the church. When the pasture is not available in the winter time or in the night, the sheep must be kept in the fold. When the pasture is ready, there is no further need for the sheep to remain in the fold. All the sheep can be led out of the fold to be gathered together as a flock to enjoy the pasture. The pasture (v. 9) signifies Christ as the feeding place for the flock. Because of this scriptural revelation, we changed the word "fold" in the chorus of this hymn to "flock."

By reading the hymns written in the last century, I discovered that many of them had the thought of going to heaven, using the Jordan River as a type of death and Canaan as a type of heaven. When I was young, I sang some of these hymns. One hymn talks about the cold waves of Jordan. When we collected some of these hymns for our hymnal, we changed this thought of going to heaven to the thought of being a victor, an overcomer.

Charles Wesley, the brother of John Wesley, was a great writer of holy songs. He wrote the hymn—"Hark! the herald angels sing." The last verse of this hymn in our hymnal says:

> Come, Desire of nations, come!
>   Fix in us Thy humble home:
> Rise, the woman's conqu'ring seed,
>   Bruise in us the serpent's head;
> Adam's likeness now efface,
>   Stamp Thine image in its place:
> Final Adam from above,
>   Reinstate us in Thy love.

In the last line of this verse, Charles Wesley used the term *Second Adam*. But 1 Corinthians 15 refers to "the last Adam" (v. 45b) and "the second Man" (v. 47). To match the truth of the Scriptures, we corrected this to read "Final Adam." We studied much to arrive at the word *final* since we had to have a two-syllable word to fit the meter.

We made these alterations to the older hymns, except where a copyright had been involved, in order to improve their accuracy in truth and enrich their spirituality in meaning. In this delicate and difficult work, we departed from the meaning and words of the original author only where it was necessary.

THE CRUCIAL POINTS
OF THE CONTENTS OF THE HYMNS

To know the hymns we have to know some of the crucial points of the contents of the hymns. First, we must know some of the hymns on the blessing and experience of the Triune God. The word *blessing* is used here not to refer to the good things the Triune God has given us but to the praise, the blessing, we offer to Him. An example of a good hymn on the blessing of the Triune God is #7—"Glory, glory, to the Father!"—and an example of a good hymn on the experience of the Triune God is #608—"What mystery, the Father, Son, and Spirit." We also need to know hymns in the categories of the praise of the Father and the praise of the Lord.

Another crucial point of the contents of the hymns is the filling of the Spirit. Some have used the term *the fullness of the Spirit*, but we have seen from the Word that fullness is used for the expression of the riches of our God. This is different from filling. The Bible reveals that there are two aspects of the filling of the Spirit—the inward filling for life and the outward filling for power. The Greek word *pleroo* refers to the inward filling and the Greek word *pletho* refers to the outward filling.

We also need to know hymns concerning the identification with Christ. I feel that *identification* is a better word than *union*. We are not just united to be together with Christ, but we are actually one with Christ. A number of hymns in this section of our hymnal were written by A. B. Simpson, the founder of the Christian and Missionary Alliance. Many of these deeper and excellent hymns written by A. B. Simpson cannot be found in today's hymnals of the Christian and Missionary Alliance churches, but we have included them in our hymnal.

The experience of Christ is another crucial point of the contents of the hymns. Hymn #499—"Oh, what a life! Oh, what a peace!"—and #501—"O glorious Christ, Savior mine" are excellent hymns in this category. We also need to know the hymns on the crucial points of the inner life, the church, the assurance of salvation, consecration, and comfort in trials. Hymn #720 is a good hymn in this section. The first verse of this hymn and the chorus read:

> God hath not promised skies always blue,
> Flower-strewn pathways all our lives through;
> God hath not promised sun without rain,
> Joy without sorrow, peace without pain.

> But God hath promised strength for the day,
> Rest for the labor, light for the way,
> Grace for the trials, help from above,
> Unfailing sympathy, undying love.

We also need to know the hymns on the crucial points of spiritual warfare, the gospel, the meetings, the hope of glory, and the ultimate manifestation. Hymn #948 and #949 are excellent hymns concerning Christ as the hope of glory, and #972 is a very good hymn on the ultimate manifestation. Hymn #949 was written to the tune of "He Lives, He Lives":

> Christ is the hope of glory, my very life is He,
> He has regenerated and saturated me;
> He comes to change my body by His subduing might
> Like to His glorious body in glory bright!

> He comes, He comes, Christ comes to glorify me!
> My body He'll transfigure, like His own it then
>   will be.
> He comes, He comes, redemption to apply!
> As Hope of glory He will come, His saints to glorify.

THE STANDARD OF THE HYMNS

We can choose three hymns from our hymnal to illustrate what we mean by the standard of the hymns— #70, #154, and #152. These hymns are concerning our love for the Lord and His love for us. The standard of hymn #70—"Oh, how I love Jesus"—is very low in life, truth, experience, and revelation. Hymn #154—"It passeth knowledge, that dear love of Thine"—is of a much higher standard. The first verse of this hymn says:

> It passeth knowledge, that dear love of Thine,
> My Savior, Jesus; yet this soul of mine
> Would of Thy love in all its breadth and length,
> Its height and depth, its everlasting strength,
> Know more and more.

Hymn #152—"O how deep and how far-reaching"—is of the highest standard. The first verse of this hymn says:

> O how deep and how far-reaching
> Is Thy love, dear Lord, to me!
> Far beyond my pow'r to fathom,
> Deeper than the deepest sea!
> It has caused Thee death to suffer
> And to me Thyself impart,
> That in Thee I might be grafted
> And become of Thee a part.

In order to know the hymns, we must know the standard of the hymns. Some hymns are of a low standard, others are of a higher standard, and others are of the very highest standard.

A. B. Simpson's hymns on the identification with Christ are of the highest standard. Hymn #481 is a very sweet song on being identified with Christ's death and resurrection. Verse 2 says:

> 'Tis not hard to die with Christ
> When His risen life we know;
> 'Tis not hard to share His suff'rings
> When our hearts with joy o'erflow.
> In His resurrection power
> He has come to dwell in me,
> And my heart is gladly going
> All the way to Calvary.

Do you feel that it is hard to die? Here is a word that tells us it is not hard to die. To die with yourself is hard, but to die with Christ is not hard. It is not hard to die with Christ "when His risen life we know." This refers to Philippians 3:10 where Paul says, "To know Him and the power of His resurrection and the fellowship of His sufferings, being conformed to His death."

Hymn #482 is another excellent hymn by A. B. Simpson on being identified with Christ's death and resurrection. I especially appreciate the third stanza:

> This the secret nature hideth,
> Harvest grows from buried grain;
> A poor tree with better grafted,
> Richer, sweeter life doth gain.

We can compare these hymns by A. B. Simpson to hymn #1059, another hymn on knowing the cross of Christ. The first verse and the chorus say:

> Jesus, keep me near the cross,
> There a precious fountain,
> Free to all—a healing stream,
> Flows from Calv'ry's mountain.

> In the cross, in the cross,
> Be my glory ever;
> From the cross my ransomed soul
> Nothing then shall sever.

The chorus of this hymn indicates that the writer was referring to Galatians 6:14—"But far be it from me to boast except in the cross of our Lord Jesus Christ, through whom the world has been crucified to me and I to the world." The word "boast" may also be translated "glory." Thus, the hymn says, "In the cross...be my glory ever." Yet this hymn does not properly convey what Paul meant in Galatians 6. Paul gloried in the cross because of the circumcision exalted by the Judaizers. The cross was really an abasement, but the apostle made it his boast. He was glorying in the shame of the cross. The most shameful death for a criminal was crucifixion. Circumcision foreshadowed the dealing with man's flesh; the cross is the reality of this dealing (Col. 2:11-12; Gal. 5:11). The Judaizers endeavored to bring the Galatians back to the shadow; the Apostle Paul struggled to keep them in the reality. Circumcision was fulfilled by Christ's crucifixion. Thus, the apostle only boasted in the cross of our Lord Jesus Christ.

This truth in Galatians is not conveyed in hymn #1059.

This hymn was written before A. B. Simpson's writings. At the time it was written, the revelation concerning the Lord's subjectiveness was not that deep. It is a good hymn, but it is obvious that the hymns by Brother Simpson are of a much higher standard.

THE SENSATION OF THE HYMNS

If we learn to sense the hymns, we can know their standard. If we sing or read a hymn, we will have a deep sensation. We can sense that #152 is deep, high, and profound. The sensation comes from the thought of the hymn. When we select a hymn for a meeting, we must do it according to our sensation based on the thought of the hymn. The sensation of a hymn also refers to its taste. Whether or not certain foods are delicious is determined by their taste. We want to know the hymns not only in an objective way but also in a subjective way by learning to taste them.

THE WORDING OF THE HYMNS

We also have to discern the wording of the hymns. Hymn #152 was written in Chinese in 1961 and translated into English. Although the English version is very good, the Chinese version is more poetic since it is easier to rhyme words in Chinese than in English. If the rhyme of a hymn is not that good and it is not that poetic, we should not choose it for our meeting. A hymn without rhyme sounds ugly. Anything that is poetic must have the proper rhyme. Some lines of certain hymns are close to rhyming, but they actually do not rhyme. *Flowed* does not rhyme with *blood* nor does *flock* rhyme with *dark*. To write a good hymn is not an easy task. A hymn must have the proper thought and proper poetic wording to take care of the rhyme and the rhythm.

THE TUNE OF THE HYMNS

The tune of the hymns is also an important aspect of our knowing the hymns. Many good hymns can be killed by a poor melody. When we compiled our hymnal, we picked up this important point of having the proper and uplifted melody for the hymns. We listened to the melodies that we selected to see whether they fit the thought and the sensation of the hymns with which they were matched. All of the new hymns written by us for our hymnal were composed with an old melody. We did not compose any new melodies. "Oh, what a life! Oh, what a peace!" was written to the tune of Charles Wesley's famous hymn— "And can it be that I should gain." This melody for #499 stirs up people's desire and feeling. I treasure many of the melodies composed in the last century and at the beginning of this century. After the second world war, most of the melodies that came out could not match those earlier sacred melodies. For instance, the tunes for "Rock of Ages" (#1058) and "Jesus, lover of my soul" (#1057) are very solid. We should try to follow that kind of style in our composing of the hymns.

In conclusion, if we are going to have meetings according to the scriptural way, we must know the hymns. We have to know the crucial points of the contents of the hymns, the standard of the hymns, the sensation of the hymns, the wording of the hymns, and the tune of the hymns. We must remember that the hymns are not only for singing, but they also are even more for speaking in the meetings. Our speaking of the proper hymns to one another and our singing of them to the Lord will enrich, enliven, uplift, refresh, and strengthen the meetings.

QUESTIONS AND ANSWERS

Question: We have been trying to write children's songs using the Scriptures to help the children memorize the Word. It is almost impossible to rhyme these songs since their content is the Scriptures themselves. How do you feel about this point?

To write songs for the children is a difficult task, but in principle, I do not agree with writing songs for them with verses from the Scripture. If we want to help the children remember some verses from the Bible, we can simply instruct them to read and recite the verses. We should not try to make the verses singable for the children. I do not mean that we should not do this at all, but this is difficult to do. To write songs for the children requires a great amount of skill. Poetry must be composed for the young ones in a very skillful way. I saw a number of songs for the children that were all below standard according to my feeling. It is better not to have songs if the songs that we have are of such a low standard.

Question: When are we going to have a revision of our hymnal? I think that our present edition has served its purpose, showing how broad and all-inclusive we are. But after twenty-two years, the standard in the Lord's recovery is much higher. I think we need a revision of the hymn book. The hymnal that we have entitled "One Hundred Selected Hymns" has been a great help to the saints. It gets them on the right track and has really uplifted the meetings. If possible, I think it would be good to have a new edition of the hymn book. How do you feel about this?

To recompile our hymnal is a hard task. In 1961 I wrote eighty-five hymns within about two months. Then in 1963 and 1964, I wrote over two hundred hymns. From that time until now, I have not had the time or the capacity to labor on the hymns. When we published our hymnal, we had the intention to show others that we knew the truth and that we were all-inclusive. In our hymnal about three hundred hymns have been written by us. The other approximately seven hundred and eighty were selected from more than eleven thousand hymns. We even selected some good hymns from the Pentecostal movement. Hymn #551 is a very good song from the Pentecostal movement. The chorus of this hymn says:

Hallelujah! Hallelujah!
I have passed the riven veil,
Here the glories never fail,
Hallelujah! Hallelujah!
I am living in the presence of the King.

Brother Nee passed on the chorus of this hymn to us in a special conference in 1934. I translated the chorus of this hymn into Chinese, and it became very popular among us for many years. When we compiled our present hymnal, we included this hymn, and we improved some of the wording so that it would be more according to the truth. Hymn #310—"Glorious freedom, wonderful freedom"—is another Pentecostal hymn that we included in our hymnal on the assurance and joy of salvation. Our hymnal has collected the best hymns from many different sources.

I agree that the purpose of our present hymnal has probably been fulfilled and that it would be good if we had a revised one. But it is very difficult to decide what hymns to drop and what hymns to keep. I wrote hymn #18 on the faithfulness of our Father God to the tune of "America the Beautiful." Even though we do not sing this hymn often, it is an excellent song on God's faithfulness, so it should not be dropped from a revised hymnal. It is hard to "draw the line" to decide which hymns to drop and which hymns to keep. Hymn #19—"Great is Thy faithfulness!"—is a very popular song, but I do not appreciate it so much in the aspect of the truth it contains. It is not that solid, complete, and perfect. Hymn #18, however, is full of truth. Every verse was written with the truth revealed in the Scriptures as a basis. This hymn begins with the universe and ends with the New Jerusalem. The rainbow around the throne and the foundation of the New Jerusalem both signify God's faithfulness. The colors of the twelve layers of the foundation give the appearance of a rainbow, signifying that the holy city is built upon and secured by God's faithfulness in keeping His covenant (Gen. 9:8-17).

If we did drop some hymns from our present hymnal, I believe that about four hundred hymns could be dropped. Although we might not use many of the remaining hymns in our meetings, we would have to keep them for the sake of the truth. We also need more hymns. In the past twenty-two years, we have received many higher visions from the Lord, but there are no hymns to match or express them.

Question: Can you fellowship with us concerning the use of the hymns in the Lord's table meeting? We have a tendency to flip from one hymn to another in the Lord's table meeting, and we sing many hymns. We can hardly consider the content of one hymn before we move to another hymn. Furthermore, our scope of knowing the hymns is very limited. We may only touch fifty or sixty hymns at the most. When I was in the Far East, I enjoyed that the saints were not in any hurry to get through the hymns in the Lord's table meeting. Two or three hymns were enough to dwell on for an entire meeting. Another thing that is troubling to me about the calling of hymns in the Lord's table is the lack of sensitivity to the flow of the meeting. Someone will call a hymn that is not according to or completely contrary to the flow. If I say that we need to change the hymn, I feel bad, but if I do not change it, the meeting suffers and many times it is impossible to bring the meeting back to the flow of the Spirit. Can you fellowship with us about the use of the hymns in the Lord's table meeting since it seems like that is where we use most of the hymns?

We must be raised up by the Lord to know the hymns. I would advise all of us to read the hymnal and become acquainted with all of the hymns. Thirty or forty years ago, we were very strict in the Lord's table. We did not allow the saints in the Lord's table to choose hymns that were far away from the purpose of the table. In the Lord's table, we remember the Lord Himself by displaying His death. We do not remember His death but we remember His very person by exhibiting, or displaying, His death. In this sense, all the hymns that are chosen and used in the Lord's table meeting should be in two categories: 1) The hymns in the Lord's table should be concerning the Lord's person and should always help people to appreciate Him. 2) We also need some hymns to show forth His death. If we can learn the hymns in our hymnal, we will be much better off in selecting the hymns.

To sing hymn after hymn in our Lord's table meeting is not good. In one Lord's table meeting it is possible to use just one hymn. In order to do this, we need to speak the hymns. Thirty or forty years ago, we were too legal. We instructed the saints strictly that they should only choose hymns in the proper category for the Lord's table meeting.

There are basically two sections to the Lord's table meeting. The first section is for remembering the Lord and the second section is for worshipping the Father. We need some discernment to choose the right hymns in the Lord's table.

I hope that we will spend some time to study the hymns. Our knowledge of the hymns will help us and will be a great help to all the meetings. It is really hard for us to adjust or correct the saints when they call an inappropriate hymn in the meeting. We may do this sometimes, but generally it is not so profitable. I hope that some leading ones in all the churches would say something concerning the hymns once a week for ten or fifteen minutes. Then the saints will gain some help for the long run and the meetings will be spontaneously adjusted and enriched.

Question: How did you write the hymns?

The secret of learning anything is to do it again and again. In learning to do something, we make mistakes, and we are perfected by learning from those mistakes. I wrote hymn #501—"O glorious Christ, Savior mine"—and then I polished, corrected, and adjusted it close to one hundred times. Now it is very hard to improve this hymn because it has been polished and adjusted to the uttermost. Some of the hymns that others among us wrote in the past were written in a quick and light way. This is not proper. The spiritual songs and hymns are the cream of a person's writing, thought, learning, life experience, and spiritual experience. If I did not have the experience of living Christ, I could not have composed that hymn—"Oh, what a life! Oh, what a peace!" That hymn is the cream of my experience, my thought, my learning, and my writing.

I would especially encourage the brothers who are forty-five or under to look to the Lord in this matter of composing the hymns. We need good composers and writers among us in the Lord's recovery. A person who is forty-five can write for twenty-five years until he is seventy. We need such people. When a hymn is written, it has to be polished, adjusted, and improved again and again. The best writers and composers use lexicons to help them. To write a hymn is a difficult task, but we need some doers in this matter.

To sing the psalms of the Old Testament is somewhat according to the Old Testament economy. We need some melodies on the book of Ephesians. We need songs on the truth from Ephesians 1:3-14 and from 3:3-11. These portions of the Word need some melodies which help the saints get into the feeling of the New Testament economy. To sing the verses from the Scriptures, we do not need to be bound. We can rewrite the verses to fit the meter and have the appropriate rhyme while maintaining the revelation and the truth that is there. We can use proper phrases from the Scriptures like "unto sonship" (Eph. 1:5) in our hymns. We need a few Charles Wesleys among us. His writings and his melodies were really marvelous. One of his great melodies is the one for "And can it be that I should gain" (#296). That melody is marvelous. A. B. Simpson is another great writer and composer of hymns that we should take as a pattern.

I want to mention again that we need to learn to speak the hymns in our meetings. This practice with Christ as the center is refreshing, nourishing, edifying, and building up. If all the saints in the Lord's recovery practiced speaking the hymns in the meetings, the meetings would be living, refreshing, and rich. This would give all the saints a way to share their enjoyment with others. We should pick up the burden to speak the hymns and endeavor to do it in our locality.

CHAPTER EIGHT

THE PRACTICE OF MEETING

(1)

In this chapter and in the next two chapters, we want to see some crucial points concerning the practice of meeting. There are a few points we need to take care of when we speak in our meetings. We must always take care of others when we speak. We have to consider whether or not people can hear our voice. We should not speak too loud or too low. Nor should we speak too fast or too slow. Furthermore, when we speak, we should do our best not to overlap others' speaking. While someone else is speaking, we should wait until they are finished before we speak. We do not need to strive or compete with others. Our speaking corporately should have a good continuation and maintain a proper order. We also need to avoid telling stories. When we share in the meetings, we are not giving a message. If a person is giving a message, he may use stories and illustrations; but in the church meeting our time is limited, and we want many to share something. We need to limit our sharing to two or three minutes so that many others have the opportunity to speak. We come to the meeting to minister Christ to others. Our speaking in the meetings must be like a composition spoken by all the attendants.

Our desire is that the saints and the churches in the Lord's recovery would be brought into a way of meeting that corresponds to the ordained way in the Bible. The practice of Christianity is traditional and follows the customs of the nations. The Bible tells us that when the church comes together, "each one has a psalm, has a teaching, has a revelation, has a tongue, has an interpretation" (1 Cor. 14:26). If we enter into the genuine practice of meeting revealed in the New Testament, our entire meeting will cover some subject or subjects that will build up the saints, the local church, and the Body of Christ.

It is difficult for a family to move to another country and change their native language. But when a family has this language laid as a foundation, all the little children in the family will spontaneously speak this language without any accent. We need to hold a strong learning spirit to learn a "new language," that is, to learn how to meet in the new way. We need to practice all the points of fellowship in this book so that our meetings can reach the goal of God's economy to build up the church.

The Lord's recovery has been among us for over sixty years, and during this time, we have learned two secrets. First, the thing that damages the meetings is our desire to "save our face" or to get some kind of glory. This is the most damaging thing and it is also deadening. If we take care of our face, we are deadened. Second, pride is a great damage to the Lord's recovery. Among us in the Lord's recovery, there are not many capable persons. Most capable persons would not come the way of the Lord's recovery because this is the way of the cross. It is a narrow and lowly way. Everyone who wants a name, a position, or a rank would not come this way. While the Lord Jesus was on this earth, He told the unbelieving Jews that He did not receive glory from men (John 5:41) and that they received glory from one another but they did not seek God's glory (v. 44). To seek man's glory is to seek some kind of rank or position. When Paul wrote his first Epistle to the church in Corinth, he addressed this matter. Corinth was a great, luxurious city in Paul's time, but Paul said that among them there were "not many wise according to flesh, not many powerful, not many wellborn" (1:26). It is the same with us today. The church of God is composed not mainly of the upper class, but of the lowborn of the world and the despised. Once one is used by the Lord, pride can come in. Actually pride is continually crouching there. If one is not a capable person, pride will not be crouching to possess him. Pride is crouching in order to gain and spoil the capable persons.

Thus, you have to put your face under your left foot and your pride under your right foot. Do not uplift your face or your pride. Put them under your feet. If these two things are under your feet, you are a victor, an overcomer. To be an overcomer, you have to overcome your face and your pride. Be careful. Once you are used and you become useful, pride is crouching there. Without the Lord's mercy in the past fifty-five years, I would have been killed by pride many times.

THE PREPARATION FOR OUR MEETING

We need to learn how to practice our meeting in a practical way. The Christian meeting is an exhibition of the Christian daily life. We need to prepare ourselves for the meetings by praying, dealing with sins, being filled with the Spirit, and abiding in the fellowship with the Lord. According to my learning and experience from the past, if we are going to meet according to the standard revealed in the Scriptures, we must be praying persons. A praying person is one who not only prays but who also has a praying spirit with a desire and an aspiration to pray. If we are this kind of person, then we are prepared to attend any kind of meeting. Whenever we are intending to go to a meeting, we must spend some time to pray for at least five to ten minutes. If we have the time, we can pray for fifteen or twenty minutes, but we should not pray too long. A longer prayer can exhaust our spirit. If I walk for two hours, my legs will become tired. Likewise, our spirit can become exhausted if we pray for too long a time before a meeting.

A proper member of a basketball team will always prepare himself for the game. He must eat properly and make sure to get enough rest. He also has to dress in the proper clothing for the game. No one would come to play in a basketball game dressed like a bank clerk. Just before the game, the player participates in certain warm-up exercises so that he is fully prepared when the game begins. In like manner, we need to be prepared for the meetings that we attend. Instead of being prepared for the church meetings, many of the saints come to the meetings in a loose way. Some even sleep in the meetings.

If a number of saints are sleeping in the meeting, that will deaden the entire meeting. Even one person who is sleeping in the meeting can frustrate the speaking spirit. If I am speaking and some of the saints are sleeping, my speaking spirit is deadened. I would not stop the meeting and ask a sleeping one to leave, but I may forget my point when I see someone sleeping and become delayed in my speaking.

When we come to the meeting, we should come to the front as fighting soldiers to conquer the enemy and as prepared athletes to win the game. If we are going to be prepared for the meetings, we must pray. I sympathize with the saints who are so busy. I am a very busy person, but I always pray before I speak. We all need such a praying spirit. We must learn to get ourselves prepared to speak in the meetings by praying.

When we pray, the Lord will show us all of our faults, shortcomings, failures, defeats, wrongdoings, and mistakes. We must deal with our sins by confessing them to the Lord. We have to make a thorough confession of all our trespasses and offenses. If we would deal with our sins thoroughly, we will enjoy the filling of the Holy Spirit. To be filled with the Holy Spirit is so normal, yet it is altogether miraculous. It is a miraculous normality. If we pray and make a thorough confession of all our sins, we will spontaneously enjoy the filling of the Holy Spirit. We realize that we are filled with the Spirit by faith, not by our feelings.

Once you have prayed and dealt with your sins to be filled with the Holy Spirit, you must learn to abide in the fellowship with the Lord. When you have prayed, dealt with your sins, and are ready to come to the meeting, it is best not to receive a phone call. Sometimes one short phone call can deaden you. The enemy tries to frustrate us either from coming to the meeting or from coming to the meeting in a prepared state. If you do not have a meeting on a particular evening, no one may call you. But when you have a meeting, a phone call may come just before you leave for the meeting. According to my experience, most of these phone calls are calls with bad news. This bad news can kill you.

It is also helpful to be careful about when you open your mail on a meeting night. Your wife may have received the mail at noon, but she forgot to tell you about a letter for you until you are ready to go to the meeting. It is best for you to put this mail aside until after the meeting. Tell Satan, "Satan, you better read the mail. This is not my business now. I'll come back after the meeting and read the mail." Many times the mail that is given to us right before the meeting has bad news to bother and frustrate us.

The husbands even have to be exercised in how they deal with their wives before the meetings. We all need to be wise by redeeming our time to keep ourselves in a good condition to attend the meeting. I hope we see that attending the meetings of the church is not a light and easy matter. For the sake of the meetings, we must learn to abide in the fellowship with the Lord.

THE STARTING OF OUR MEETING

The proper starting of our meeting should not be in the meeting hall but in our homes. We should start the meeting by calling on the Lord's name, praying, singing, praising, and speaking. While we are on the way to the meeting place and when we arrive, we can continue to enjoy the Lord in this way. If a number of the saints are already there practicing the meeting, we can join what they are already doing.

THE SUBJECT OF OUR MEETING

In our meetings we do not need to have a definite subject. To have a definite subject is wrong according to the revelation of 1 Corinthians 14:26, which says that whenever we come together, each one has a psalm, has a teaching, has a revelation, has a tongue, or has an interpretation. Surely each attendant will not bring something to the meeting that covers the same subject. Hebrews

10:25 also implies this. This verse tells us that in our meetings we need to "exhort one another." How could the meeting have a definite subject when we are exhorting one another? There is no need of a definite subject in our meetings. We need to keep the meeting open to any subject or subjects as the Lord leads through the attending saints. Our meetings do not need a prearranged program. We must have the faith to have our meetings with nothing prearranged. Having a program binds, annuls, and kills.

A rich feast is composed not only of one dish. The more courses of food there are and the more variety there is, the richer the feast is. Some leading ones have made some prior arrangements when the saints come together for a love feast. They assign certain saints to bring hot food, others to bring salad, others to bring bread, and others to bring potatoes. But this is not a real feast. A feast has more than just four courses. It should have at least twelve courses with many varieties of foods and tastes. Such a feast is a real enjoyment, and a rich meeting should be just like this. Each saint should bring a different "dish." Our meetings need to be a real feast to both God and man. We all need to bring our topmost portion of the riches of Christ that we have enjoyed to the church meeting and present them for God's satisfaction and the saints' nourishment. I believe the Lord's recovery will arrive at the reality of 1 Corinthians 14:26 because this is the Lord's Word. This is the heavenly and divine way revealed in the Scriptures. We must take care of what is said in the Holy Bible. First Corinthians 14:26 does tell us that whenever we come together, each one should have something. Throughout the years of the Lord's recovery, some of us have tasted and experienced some meetings in the nature of what is revealed in 1 Corinthians 14:26. Now the Lord wants us to enter into the full reality of such a wonderful meeting life.

THE GOAL OF OUR MEETING—TO EXHIBIT CHRIST

The goal of our meeting is to exhibit Christ, and the Christian meeting is an exhibition of the Christian daily life. The Christian daily life is just Christ. Paul said, "For to me to live is Christ" (Phil. 1:21a). Christ must be our daily life, and our meeting is an exhibition, a display, of our daily life. The center of this display is Christ Himself. Whatever we pray, speak, or sing must be with Christ as the center. We do not speak other things. We only speak Christ. We must learn to practice our meetings according to the scriptural way of meeting and serving. We cannot practice the new way according to our natural way. We must be trained in the spirit and with the Word.

THE PURPOSE OF OUR MEETING—
TO BUILD UP THE SAINTS
FOR THE BUILDING UP OF THE BODY OF CHRIST

The purpose of our meeting is to build up the saints for the building up of the Body of Christ. According to my observation, many Christian meetings, or so-called services, at the very most only help to edify the saints without building up the Body. To build up the Body of Christ as an organism, we need the meetings which are according to the Bible. The unscriptural, traditional way of meeting annuls, chokes, and deadens the living members of the Body of Christ.

One can build an article of furniture by arranging and attaching pieces of wood to one another in an organizational way. But to build up a person as an organism is a different matter. Whatever is put into a person to build him up must be something living, something of life. For a living person to be built up, he needs to take in some organic, living substance. Morticians make corpses look better by putting make-up on them. Although a corpse may look better outwardly, it is still full of death. The Lord's way is not to change us only outwardly but to add His very life into our inward being to transform us and make us His living members.

Death is more defiling before God than sin (Lev. 11:24-25; Num. 6:6-7, 9). According to the Old Testament, if anyone sinned, he could be forgiven simply by offering the sin offering (Lev. 4:27-31). However, anyone who touched the dead body of a man had to wait seven days before he could be cleansed (Num. 19:11, 16). The traditional way of meeting is a way of death. We must practice the new way of meeting according to the Bible. We must stay away from any way that is deadening, annulling, or choking and take the way that supplies people with something organic and that builds up an organism, not an organization. The reason why the Lord has not come back yet is because there is not such a living organism on this earth to match Him.

There are hundreds of millions of Christians on this earth today, but where is the Body built up? There are thousands and thousands of assemblies and gatherings, but where can we see the organic Body? We cannot see the organic Body of Christ because the meetings in the traditional way cannot fulfill God's purpose to build up the Body. Week after week many believers attend this kind of meeting, but at best they are only edified personally. Only the way to meet that is according to the Bible can build up the Body of Christ as a divine organism.

Whatever we do in the scriptural way of meeting requires the exercise of our spirit. If we speak, read, sing, or testify, we must exercise our spirit. When we exercise our spirit, the Spirit that is within our spirit operates and the issue is something organic. This is why we should not behave, act, or move in the meeting according to anything natural. We must do everything according to our spirit under the anointing. Then something organic will come out to nourish us and others in order to build up the organic Body of Christ. In our meetings the saints are built up for the building up of the Body of Christ by four things: by our giving a testimony, speaking forth Christ, teaching the truth, and preaching the gospel. These are four categories of things that we can and should cover in our meetings.

QUESTIONS AND ANSWERS

Question: Could you give a little more explanation regarding not needing a prearranged program for our meetings?

Quite often in the church, we need to call a special gathering. Every special gathering has a special purpose and for that gathering we need a definite subject, a definite program, and even some prearrangement as to who will bear the burden for this meeting. But for the regular meetings of the church, there should not be a prearranged program or a definite subject. We should come together and leave the entire meeting to the guiding Spirit.

Question: Suppose some saints want to come together to go over a truth lesson. That is a definite subject. How does this fit in with what we are seeing regarding the meetings not needing to have a definite subject?

This is a very good question. All the saints need to learn the crucial truths in the Scriptures. For the long run, a local church must have a time, either weekly, bi-weekly, or at least monthly, to have a meeting for the teaching of the truth to the saints. This kind of teaching of the truth should not depend upon what we call regular church meetings. The publication that can help us learn the truths to the uttermost is *Truth Lessons*. In using the *Truth Lessons* we should not follow the traditional way. We must take the new way of practicing the learning of the *Truth Lessons*.

Even with this matter, we should not be too definite regarding what or how much we will cover in the meeting. We may have made a prior decision to cover a certain truth lesson in a meeting. But when we come together, we may realize that this lesson is too long. We may be able to cover this entire lesson in four meetings. Thus, when we come together, an instant decision may come out, and we may decide to only cover the first part or the first few pages.

Someone may even be burdened to cover the final fourth of the lesson. We should go along with this proposal. We may wonder how we could cover the fourth part when we have not covered the previous three parts. But quite often we can learn more this way. I am sharing this to impress us that it is better not to control, limit, or restrict the saints that much. It is always a profit to keep the meeting open and depend on the Lord's instant leading. But on the other hand, we should not be too loose. If we are too loose, many opinions will come out.

A sister who was a medical doctor once came to me and told me that our church needed a hospital, and she encouraged me to promote this matter. Some people who are Ph.D.'s may feel that we need to establish some schools. These are opinions from the natural man. We should not be too loose in the meetings. Otherwise, the door will be open for many opinions. We have to learn to restrict and limit this element, but we should not be too strict or controlling. In other words, there are actually no regulations, but we are always under God's guidance and leading.

Question: I have been in some localities that practice getting into a certain book of the Bible with the help of the Life-study Messages. They come together for a meeting of fellowship, and the content of this meeting is usually what the saints have labored on with the Life-studies. What do you feel about this practice?

A lame person who wants to walk may need a cane to help him. When the strength and health of his legs are eventually recovered, though, he will no longer need this cane. Likewise, when we start to practice the new way, we may need a little help. But eventually when everybody is regularly contacting the Lord and having enjoyment in the word, they will gain an accumulation of the experiences of Christ and a living storage of the living word of Christ. Thus, everyone will be rich. When we come together in this state, everyone will have something to present from the storehouse in his being.

Probably right now many of us do not have any "savings." We only have a "checking account" with one dollar and fifty cents. If we practice the new way, however, eventually, perhaps within six months, we will all have some savings. Then it will be easy for us to "write checks" in the meetings. Thus, we need to prepare. Because we may only have one dollar and fifty cents in our checking account now, we may need to borrow something by using the Life-studies, the *Truth Lessons*, or the *Life Lessons* in the regular church meetings. There is nothing wrong with this. But we must learn to bring the saints into a stage where they can drop all the "canes" and the helps because they have the accumulation of the experiences of Christ and the riches of the truth from the living word of Christ. If we continue to take the scriptural way, we will reach a stage where most of the saints are rich in the experience of Christ and in the enjoyment of the word. Then when we come together, it will be easy to have a rich feast with many courses. To use something like the Life-studies is not wrong, but be careful that the saints do not build up a habit of relying on this too much. Otherwise, they may not have a desire to contact the Lord in the morning to accumulate some riches. They may build up a habit of only preparing a little bit on the assigned pages of a certain book. That is not good for the long run and builds up a bad habit.

CHAPTER NINE

THE PRACTICE OF MEETING

(2)

In this chapter we want to continue our fellowship concerning the practice of meeting. In particular, we want to cover some crucial points concerning our need to pay full attention to the way of speaking.

GETTING YOURSELF PREPARED
TO SPEAK IN THE MEETING

We must pay our full attention to the way of speaking. If we are going to speak properly, we must get ourselves prepared to speak in the meeting. Unless we are burdened to speak or assigned to speak, we may not have any thought to speak in the meeting. Our thought is that somebody else will speak and that we do not need to speak. If you have been a Christian for twenty years and have attended three meetings a week, you have been in about three thousand meetings. On these three thousand occasions, how many times did you consider speaking in the meeting? Possibly you never once considered that you needed to speak. There was always someone there to speak for you. For this reason it is hard for us to change our way today. Our speaking function has been annulled. If a child is not given any opportunity to speak for twenty years, he will be dumb. His speaking function will be annulled by his lack of speaking and practicing. This illustrates our problem today. We have so many saints among us today who love the Lord and are faithful to the Lord's testimony. However, some who have been among us for many years have been annulled due to the old way of meeting.

When we do speak, we must learn how to speak properly. We must all practice and learn. Over fifty years ago Brother Watchman Nee, the pioneer in the Lord's recovery among us, saw the light concerning the way to meet. He put what he saw into printed messages, yet we did not find a way to practice it. We had nothing with which to replace our old way of one man speaking in the meetings. Now we have been in the line of the recovery for over sixty years, and we have had much practice and experience. By the Lord's mercy, we have published a number of books concerning the scriptural way of meeting. Now we have a way. We also have many publications in truth and in life. These publications are a great storage of "groceries." Our only need is to learn how to cook them.

Whenever you attend a meeting, the first thought you should have is to speak. Get prepared to speak. Whether the actual time for you to speak will come or not is another matter, but you must have the thought to speak. To go to the meeting is to go to speak. To go to a meeting is not to go to listen. To go to a feast is not to go to look at the feast or talk about the feast. At a feast the main thing is to eat. Therefore, the first item of the proper way of speaking is to get yourself prepared to speak in the meeting.

NOT OVERLAPPING OTHERS' SPEAKING

When we speak, we should not overlap others' speaking. There should be no overlapping but rather a good continuation from one person's speaking to the next person's speaking. One speaks while all the others wait; then the next one speaks. Between the preceding speaking and your speaking there must be a little *selah* as in the Psalms. Stop for a while; it is more meaningful. Then you will have a good continuation. There will not be noise, but a proper voice in a good continuation. Although this may not be too easy with a hundred or a thousand meeting together, the meeting should still have a good sequence and a good continuation.

NOT TOO LOW OR TOO SLOW, NEITHER TOO LOUD NOR TOO FAST

Our speaking should not be too low without loving the audience's ears. You may love your throat too much.

Instead, you should love others' ears. Learn to speak audibly. You must sound out your voice that it may be audible. You are not speaking to yourself; you are speaking to others. We should also not speak too slow to exhaust the audience's patience. To speak too low or too slow is not good. We all have to hate these two ways of speaking. Furthermore, we should not speak too loud to hurt the audience's ears, nor should we speak too fast to puzzle the audience. Often I was puzzled at someone's speaking. I could not follow it.

We must learn not to speak too low or too slow; neither should we speak too loud nor too fast. We may learn to speak properly in our homes by ourselves. We mean business in these matters. Our Christian life is altogether focused on the meeting life. If there were no meeting life, there would be no Christian life. These matters are quite important and are worthy of our study.

BY EXERCISING YOUR SPIRIT ALL THE WAY

We should speak by exercising our spirit all the way. Many times when we speak, we disregard our spirit. During the course of our speaking, we may only exercise our spirit when we come to a point which we prefer. Our speaking, however, should not change like the seasons. When we open our mouths to speak, we must exercise our spirits from the first word. Otherwise, we are not qualified to speak. We must speak all the way not only in our spirit but also by exercising our spirit. This is important and it makes a difference.

To exercise your spirit does not always mean that you shout. By your experience you know what it is to speak without the spirit, and you also know what it is to speak with the spirit. These points for our speaking require our exercise and practice.

AVOIDING TELLING SEA STORIES

In our speaking we should avoid telling "sea stories." Some try to lay a foundation for the point they are trying to make by telling a long story, and many times they do this without hitting the subject of their testimony. You do not need to tell these sea stories. To give a testimony is not to give a message. In giving a testimony about your history with the Lord you may simply say three sentences. This is enough to cover the entire story. Then the listeners will be happy. They will not be so heavily burdened with a long sea story.

Sometimes the brothers may have to tell the person who is giving a sea story to stop and give time for others to share. It is very hard and not so polite to stop someone while they speak in the meeting. This always hurts people's feelings. However, everyone should consider that there may only be an hour and a half for many people to speak, and a sea story takes too much time. We have seen some who speak in a lengthy way in every meeting they attend. It seems that they have no sensation of time; they only care for their speaking. We are not outside of time. We must care for the hours, minutes, and seconds. We must learn to be limited by time.

AVOIDING ERRORS IN TRUTH

We must avoid errors in truth when we speak. It is very easy for us to be mistaken. I may make mistakes in my speaking, but I will not publish any message without polishing or revising it. In this polishing and revising, I make many corrections. Learn to speak the truth. If you do not have the assurance in giving numbers or other details, you had better not do it.

AVOIDING EXPOSING OTHERS

Avoid exposing others in your speaking. It is easy for us to expose someone, even in our testimony, but it is altogether not profitable or helpful. It only damages the situation.

AVOIDING ANGER IN SPEAKING

You must avoid anger in speaking. If you are angry, you must not speak. Speaking in anger kills the situation and kills your speaking spirit. Sometimes someone may interrupt your speaking. This may easily make you angry, but learn to hold back your anger, and never speak in anger. At other times someone in the audience may ask you a very peculiar question while you speak. This kind of peculiar question also stirs up people's anger. Some who listen to your speaking may not like it and may rise up and walk out. Do not be bothered or touched by that. When you are speaking, do not let anything bother you. Do not focus your attention on any distracting element in the meeting. Continue to speak in a pleasant way, avoiding anger in your speaking.

AVOIDING LENGTHY SPEAKING

Try to avoid lengthy speaking. This does not mean that you should speak in such a short way that people will have difficulty understanding you. Your speaking should be very easy for people to understand. Some brothers and sisters speak like they are sending a telegram. This is wrong. It is better to lengthen this kind of speaking, but if you speak too long, this is also not good.

SEEING THE VISION
AND BEING BURDENED FOR THE NEW WAY

If we have seen that the new way to meet is better than the old way, we must endeavor to learn and practice this way and help others to do the same. We need much learning. We should pick up the burden to practice the new way with patience with ourselves and with others. In any aspect of human society it is not an easy thing to change a habitual way. This is true not only in a church like that in Taipei with about ten thousand people, but also in a church of only one hundred people. Even in a family of eight it is not easy to change a habit.

Some Chinese families living in the United States may find it hard to drop their habit of eating with chopsticks. Two members of the family may want to use forks, but the rest may insist on using chopsticks. They would say that without chopsticks the flavor in eating is spoiled and that with them every course tastes so good. To put away the old

way of meeting and pick up this biblical way is a great
change. Some older brothers and sisters and even some
young ones who have been with us for a few years may not
feel so happy about it. They may feel somewhat awkward.
Therefore, we must see the vision of the scriptural way to
meet and to serve for the building up of the Body of Christ.
We must take this new way or the Lord will have no way to
go on.

In the way of Christianity how could the Lord edify His
members organically for the development of their organic
function that they may build up an organism, the Body of
Christ? There is no possibility. We have studied and
investigated and have seen that the Body of Christ cannot
be built up in the old way of Christianity. At most an
organized "church," a group of people organized together,
can be built up. However, that is not something organic. To
build up an organism in an organic way we need all the
spiritual organs of the saints to be developed. Therefore,
we must take the new way. Sooner or later, if not at this
time then in the following years, the Lord will work this
out. He needs some to take this new way.

Two thousand years have passed and there is no Body
of Christ as an organism which is built up. According to
the record of the New Testament, the church at the time of
the apostles was not better than it is today. At that time
Paul suffered much. It was he who pioneered the way to
bring the gospel to all of Asia Minor, and it was he who
taught the saints there. He stayed in Ephesus for three
years (Acts 19:1, 22; 20:31). He did much for the churches in
Asia and wrote some epistles to them. However, by the
time of his martyrdom, all who were in Asia forsook him
with his ministry (2 Tim. 1:15) due mainly to different
opinions. A proper Body of Christ was not built up at
Paul's time, at the beginning of the church age. The seven
epistles from the Lord to the churches in Asia confirm this
(Rev. 2:1—3:22).

Two thousand years have passed and what is here
today? Where is the built up Body of Christ? We must
believe that the Lord Jesus cannot be defeated. He will

surely do something. He is able. The reason He has tolerated the situation is that He would not do anything by Himself with His divine power alone. He likes to do things in the principle of incarnation. The principle of incarnation is that the divine power must be mingled with the human element. He needs us. On the side of the divine power, there has been no problem. Even two thousand years ago there was no problem. The problem is on our side, the human side. On the human side the greatest problem is the different human opinions.

We should not expect that since the Lord has shown us this new way and we have brought the new way into the recovery, all the churches will be happy to take it. To think this way is somewhat childish. Do not forget that we all are still human. Therefore, there is the need of some faithful ones, who have seen the vision and the need, to pick up the burden to pray. Prayer is first. Then we have to do something like the apostles, who were pioneers and good examples.

QUESTIONS AND ANSWERS

Question: What is the difference between overlapping someone's speaking and emphasizing a certain point?

Regardless of how much you would emphasize any point, you should not speak it by overlapping others' speaking. You must wait until others finish their speaking. Then you may utter something. It is not good to have two speakings overlapping each other.

Question: If something is spoken that is incorrect according to the truth, should we let it go or should we correct the speaker in the meeting?

Errors in the truth are in degrees. If the error is to a serious degree, such as denying the deity of the Lord Jesus, it must be adjusted immediately in the meeting for it concerns our basic faith. On the other hand, a mistake in numbers, such as saying that the Lord fed five thousand in Matthew 15 rather than four thousand, should be let go. To correct people in the meeting is not pleasant. You should avoid doing this unless the mistake is serious and concerns basic truths. If the mistake is serious and concerns basic truths, we should correct the error immediately in order to let people know what our faith is.

In other cases in which an error is made in a person's testimony, the correction should not be made immediately after the testimony. If you do this, that person may be offended. You may feel to correct the person, but many others may feel that it is better not to correct him. We all have to exercise our love. To stop a speaker who makes errors may not only offend him but may offend the other saints as well. It is better to wait until another meeting. In another meeting you may give a little message telling the saints to learn how to follow the trend in the meeting. Give them some illustrations and examples. That will spontaneously correct and change the way of meeting.

CHAPTER TEN

THE PRACTICE OF MEETING

(3)

In this chapter we want to continue our fellowship regarding our need to pay full attention to the way of speaking.

TAKING CHRIST AS THE CENTER
AND ELEMENT OF YOUR SPEAKING

Whenever we speak, either in or outside of the meetings, we should take Christ as the center and element. This requires much practice and experience. If we give a testimony, give a short message, or sing a hymn, we must take Christ as the center. Christ must be the focus, the very center, the element, and the substance of our speaking. Even when a person speaks in a secular way, his speaking has an element and a substance. The things of the world or our own history, the story concerning ourselves, may be the substance of our speaking instead of Christ. In the church we should always take Christ as the very constituting element, composing substance, and content of our speaking.

In our prayer we must also take Christ as the center and element. We must train ourselves to do this. As human beings, we are accustomed to talking in a very secular, common, and worldly way. This is because we are short of the knowledge and experience of Christ, and even though we may have some experience of Christ, we are still short of the utterance of Christ. Our utterances may be so secular, worldly, and common. To use such utterances is to reduce the value of Christ and eliminate the very effectiveness of Christ's work. Therefore, we must learn to pick up some expressions and utterances, either from the Bible or from highly valued spiritual writings. This means that we must learn the spiritual content of certain spiritual books.

We also should study the Bible and read the hymns. Spontaneously we will accumulate a good vocabulary to express our knowledge concerning Christ and our experience of Christ.

Even if we have the knowledge and experience of Christ and we have the proper vocabulary, we still need to learn to mingle our words, our speaking, with Christ. A brother may give a testimony concerning how he dealt with a troublesome taxicab driver. But as a Christian and one that is learning to live Christ, his story should be something mingled with Christ. He may say, "Today I had trouble with a cab driver, but Christ within me told me that I had to tolerate him. The more I considered before the Lord, the more I felt that the Lord wanted me to pay him whatever he asked." By telling a story in this way, he mingles his speaking with Christ and applies Christ as the element in his speaking.

In giving a message or a testimony, one may speak merely in a common way without the mingling of Christ. This is poor. To take Christ as the center and element of our speaking does not mean simply to choose a topic concerning Christ. If we do not have the assurance that we have Christ as the center and element of our speaking, it is better not to speak. Do not speak anything without Christ.

A person may give even a biblical teaching without Christ. This is wrong. In our meetings we do not want any speaking in a testimony, message, or exhortation without Christ. Even the teachers of Confucianism give good exhortations without Christ. We should not forget that we have been gathered by the Lord out of every kind of occupation into His name, and we are now meeting in His name with Him. Therefore, Christ as everything to us must be the element and focus of our speaking. Our speaking should not be apart from Christ. Without Christ, we cannot speak properly in a Christian meeting.

LOOKING TO THE LORD FOR INSTANT AND FRESH ENLIGHTENMENT, VISION, AND UTTERANCE

If we take Christ as the center and element of our

speaking, we will spontaneously look to the Lord for instant and fresh enlightenment, vision, and utterance. All Christian believers are priests. As a priest you should not teach common things or use common words, utterances, points, or illustrations. Learn to speak as a Christian priest. We are all members of the Body, and we are all priests in the church serving our Lord in a particular, separated, and sanctified way. Therefore, while we are speaking anything, we must look to Him for further inspiration and utterance.

I can testify that when I give a message, I look to the Lord that He would give me the instant and fresh utterance and also the fresh enlightenment and vision. Many times while I am speaking, new light comes to enlighten me, and I see something new which is the instant vision. There was a kind of instant view seen by me through the Lord's enlightening while I was speaking. I may prepare an outline for my message, but when I speak, something new comes that is not on the outline.

The constant word is solid, but the instant utterance always inspires people to the uttermost. The power is not mainly in the constant word but in the instant utterance. We need to have the constant utterance as a base since our speaking should be built upon some constant understanding and knowledge. But the constant utterance alone cannot work out much in a meeting. If we are going to stir up and inspire people, we must have the instant utterance, the utterance that comes to us at the moment. Once we have the instant utterance, our speaking becomes powerful. Andrew Murray once said that a powerful and unlimited speaker always has some instant utterance, something new. If we only speak what we have prepared as an old foundation, this will not be so adequate. Every good speaker must look to the Lord for some fresh utterance and some fresh new light.

The things of the scriptural way will not be hard if we practice them. If we love Christ, love the church, and love the Christian experience, the scriptural practice will not be a hardship to us. If we have a heart for the Lord and the church, we will not feel that anything concerning God's economy is a hardship. A nursing mother cherishes her little babe. Because of her heart for this little one, she does not consider her sacrifice as a hardship. We need a heart that seeks after the Lord and that loves the Lord. At the end of the Gospel of John, the Lord Jesus asked Peter three times if he loved Him (John 21:15-17) because our life with the Lord needs such a love.

At the end of the book of Ephesians, Paul said, "Grace be with all those who love our Lord Jesus Christ in incorruption" (6:24). For the proper church life, we need to love the Lord in incorruptibility, which is to love the Lord in and according to all the crucial items revealed and taught in the six chapters of Ephesians. These crucial items, such as the Body of Christ, the new man, the economy of God's mystery, the oneness of the Spirit, truth and grace, light and love, as well as each item of God's armor, etc., are all incorruptible. For the church our love for the Lord must be in these incorruptible things. When we love the Lord in these incorruptible things, not one of them will be hard to us. The new man is a wonderful, deep, and unfathomable item of God's economy, but if we love the Lord in the incorruptible new man, the new man becomes an easy item to us.

Spiritual things seem very hard for some to grasp because they do not love the deep things of God. When you talk to some people about these things, you feel as if you are playing fine music to a cow. The cow does not have an ear for fine music. However, to those of us who have a heart for the Lord and the deep things of God, messages on these spiritual things are like beautiful melodies. When I was young, I remember listening to a message given in the Spirit and feeling that it was beautiful music. It sounded so pleasant to me and was so easy to understand. As those who have a heart for the Lord, we need to learn to look to the Lord for His instant, refreshing enlightenment that we may have a new vision to speak with new utterances.

TRUSTING IN THE LORD'S SPEAKING
WITHIN YOUR SPEAKING

We also need to trust in the Lord's speaking within our speaking. While I am speaking, I trust that within my speaking the Lord speaks. Actually, my speaking in itself means nothing. The real power and impact of my speaking is the Lord's speaking in my speaking. My speaking is a shell; it may be likened to a box that contains a diamond. Little children who do not realize the value of a diamond might treasure the box that contains the diamond more than the diamond itself. If you are childish, you may treasure my speaking. But the experienced saints can sense that there is a treasure within my speaking, and that treasure is the Lord's speaking.

When Brother Watchman Nee was a young man, M. E. Barber, an older sister in the Lord, helped him to the uttermost. Brother Nee went with Sister Barber a number of times to hear certain preachers and Bible teachers. After a message, which Brother Nee thought was wonderful, he asked Sister Barber what she thought. Sister Barber told him that the message was an empty shell full of eloquence without the content of life. In other words, within the person's eloquent speaking there was not the Lord's speaking. This happened quite often with Brother Nee and Sister Barber. One day they went to listen to an ineloquent speaker of whom Brother Nee had a very poor impression. After his message, Sister Barber told Brother Nee that this person had something of Christ and the cross. By this Brother Nee learned to take care of the treasure in a person's speaking. When we speak, we should look to the Lord that in our speaking He would speak.

The Lord Jesus indicated that when He spoke, the Father within Him was working. He said, "The words which I speak to you, I do not speak from Myself; but the Father who abides in Me, He does His works" (John 14:10). The Lord Jesus also said, "The word which you hear is not Mine, but the Father's who sent Me" (v. 24). The Lord Jesus had the attitude that His speaking would have been vain and empty if the Father did not speak in His speaking or if

He spoke without the Father's working. The Lord never spoke His own word. He always spoke the Father's word. What a pattern to us!

We may not be required to speak for ten or twenty minutes in the meetings, but even if we only speak for two or three minutes, we have to look to the Lord for His speaking within our speaking. We have to learn this lesson whenever we speak in the meetings. We should pray, "Lord, if You would not speak in my speaking, I would not speak." If we learn these points concerning the way of speaking and practice them, the church meetings will be very much uplifted and enriched. We cannot take the traditional way of coming to the meetings unprepared without any consideration or sensation. We should not come to the meeting merely to fulfill our duty. This is wrong. All of us have to get ourselves prepared to speak in the meetings and look to the Lord for His speaking in our speaking.

FOLLOWING THE ANOINTING OF THE LORD

When we speak, we also must follow the anointing of the Lord. The Lord's inner anointing is the moving of the Holy Spirit as the ultimate consummation of the processed Triune God. If we follow the inner anointing in our speaking, that anointing will become the Lord's speaking. The Lord's speaking is the anointing within us.

BEING EMPOWERED BY
THE SPIRIT OF POWER IN YOUR SPEAKING

The Lord's anointing, the Lord's speaking, and power in our speaking are the same thing. The Lord's speaking is the anointing, and the anointing is the power in which we are empowered. This gives us the impact in our speaking.

ENDEAVORING TO SPEAK EVERYTHING WITH A VERSE
OR A PORTION OF THE SCRIPTURE AS ITS BASE

We need to endeavor to speak everything in the meetings with a verse or a portion of the Scripture as its base. Our speaking must be based upon the Scripture.

Thus, it is always good to pick up an appropriate verse to match our speaking. The Lord's speaking, the anointing, the power, and an appropriate verse from the Bible are all one. When all these elements are present, the word that we speak is the living Triune God. Our speaking must always be mingled and blended with the Triune God through the Spirit in His Word.

ENDEAVORING TO TAKE CARE OF THE FLOW AND ATMOSPHERE OF THE MEETING

Whenever we meet, we have the assurance of the Lord's promise that He is with us (Matt. 18:20). The Bible reveals that, as the Spirit, He is the breath and the wind. In John 3 the Greek word *pneuma* is translated into spirit (v. 6) and wind (v. 8). Whether *pneuma* means wind or spirit depends upon the context. Verse 8 says that it blows, and the sound of it can be heard. This indicates that it is the wind. A regenerated person is like the wind, which can be realized, but which is beyond understanding. The very Lord who is with us in our meetings is like the breath and the wind. On the day of Pentecost, the Spirit was like a rushing violent wind that filled the room where the believers were (Acts 2:2, 4). The Triune God was in that blowing wind because He Himself is the wind, the air, and the breath. In the Old Testament, the Hebrew word *ruach* can be translated into wind, breath, or spirit. In Ezekiel 37 *ruach* is translated in these three ways (vv. 5, 9, 14).

We believe that whenever we meet in the name of the Lord, He is with us as the air and the wind. The wind blows and flows. In the meeting there is a spiritual flow, and we must learn how to follow this flow. The Spirit may be flowing in a certain direction in a meeting, but we may behave against the flow and miss it. The flow always goes together with the atmosphere. The atmosphere of the meeting is the issue of the flow. Someone's speaking in a meeting may stop the flow of the meeting, and the entire meeting may be brought out of the flow and its accompanying atmosphere. Thus, we must learn to follow the flow and atmosphere of the meeting.

AVOIDING SPEAKING MERELY DOCTRINES,
THOUGH SCRIPTURAL

In our meetings we should avoid speaking merely doctrines, though scriptural. We do not want mere doctrines without some reality for the Christian experience and without the supply of life. When we speak, we should minister the Spirit and the divine life into others.

AVOIDING REFERRING TO SECULAR STORIES,
ILLUSTRATIONS, AND PARABLES

When we speak, we should also avoid referring to secular stories, illustrations, and parables. Because we were raised up, educated, and instructed in many ways in human society, we have a tendency to speak secular things. But in the church meetings we are speaking for the Lord. It is hard for us to keep our speaking away from secular stories, illustrations, and parables. Whenever we use secular things in our speaking, we eliminate the power and the impact of our speaking. This is a subtraction from our speaking. When we speak, we have to do it without any reference to secular things.

AVOIDING QUOTATIONS
FROM BOOKS WITHOUT SPIRITUAL WEIGHT

We should avoid quoting things from books without spiritual weight. Many times people like to quote from others' books in their speaking because they think that these quotations can strengthen or confirm their points. They also may quote others to strengthen or confirm that they are learned and knowledgeable. We do not need to make such a show of our knowledge of others' books. To refer to others' books is a risk. We may bring in things that are not according to the truth or that are not constructive. Our speaking with wrong quotations from others' books may distract others and destroy our intention to build up the church. To bring in quotations from other books may even create dissension, so we have to be careful when we quote others' writings.

AVOIDING MENTIONING PEOPLE'S NAMES
AS MUCH AS POSSIBLE

We need to avoid mentioning people's names as much as possible in the meeting. Unless it is necessary for some reason, it is much better not to relate negative stories. If it is really needed, we may refer to negative stories, but it is altogether wrong to mention people's names. Even in giving a positive story or testimony concerning a certain person or persons, it is also wise not to mention their names, if possible, that we may stay away from exalting people and from making mistakes.

AVOIDING LIBERAL AND WRONG INTERPRETATIONS
OF THE HOLY WORD

We should also avoid liberal and wrong interpretations of the holy Word. In our speaking, especially in public meetings, when we interpret any part of the holy Word, either a single word, a phrase, a clause, a sentence, a paragraph, a chapter, or a book, we must not take the liberal way as some of the liberal translations. Also we must do our best to avoid wrong, erroneous, and mistaken definitions and significances.

AVOIDING SPEAKING
A NUMBER OF UNRELATED POINTS
WITHOUT A SUBSTANTIAL EMPHASIS

Whenever we speak in the meetings, we must avoid speaking a number of unrelated points without a substantial emphasis. There was a dear brother among us in the church in Shanghai about fifty years ago. Whenever he spoke, he had many good points. However, one of the elders in the church said, "Every sentence that this brother speaks is a treasure, but when these sentences are put together, they mean nothing." We must always try to speak with some definite emphasis; otherwise, our speaking will be minimized.

AVOIDING ANY KIND OF DEBATE, ARGUMENT,
OR DEPRECIATION OF OTHERS' SPEAKING

We should never debate, argue, or depreciate others'

speaking in the meetings. People do have a tendency to debate with others. There was one brother among us who was strong in his opinion. If the fellowship was to "go west," he would go "east." When we dealt with this brother, we exercised much wisdom. If we intended to go west, we would say we needed to go east. He would disagree with this and say that we needed to go west. Then we would go west. This brother just liked to go contrary to whatever anyone else felt. Some of us may be in this category of liking to debate or argue. If the opportunity arises in a meeting, some may say, "I don't agree with you, brother." That kills the entire meeting. To have a living Christian meeting, we must avoid any kind of debate or argument. We should also not belittle anyone or depreciate others' speaking.

QUESTIONS AND ANSWERS

Question: What is the difference between reading something in the meeting and speaking it?

Too much analysis of this matter does not help. We need to endeavor in a simple way not merely to read but to speak. By our practice we will learn how to speak the hymns or perhaps to speak something from the printed publications of the ministry. We should not analyze what it is to speak, talk, read, or declare something in the meetings. All these things are very close. Speaking the printed material is very close to reading and declaring. But there is a difference. Reading is more according to the letter, while speaking is more free, automatic, and spontaneous. Often you may not speak exactly what is printed. You can add a few words which do not affect the meaning. We need to practice speaking so that we can enter into the full reality of the new way in our meeting life. The more that we practice speaking, the more we will learn.

How much better the meetings in the new way are than the old message meetings depends upon our practice. Our practice in the meetings may be compared to a basketball game. If you put a basketball in my hands, I could not play well with it. But if you give the same ball to five trained players, they will play in a skillful way. To play ball we need certain skills; without learning them we can never function skillfully. The success of the game depends on the players. Christianity, however, has annulled the function of the members of Christ by building up one speaker as the "coach" to "play ball" by himself.

To meet together in the biblical way should be easier today than at the apostles' time. At the time of the apostles the believers did not yet have the completed New Testament. They only had the Old Testament and some songs and hymns. Today, however, we not only have the Old Testament but also the New Testament. We may speak directly from the Bible in a meeting. To speak from the Bible is more than adequate for a meeting because the Bible was written in such a spiritual, economical, and rich way. No one can speak a message that can compare to any page of the Bible. We also have a good hymnal and a number of good books, such as *Truth Lessons*, *Life Lessons*, the Life-study Messages, *The Experience of Life*, *The Economy of God*, and *The All-Inclusive Christ*. We may bring any of these books to the meeting, and when we open them, something marvelous will be there. We do not necessarily need to speak starting from the first section of a chapter, but we can use any page. We may "play ball" from any section. In a meeting you may say, "Let us read a section of *Life Lessons* concerning the two aspects of the Spirit." Or you may say, "Let us speak the nine titles of the Spirit as listed in this section."

We have spent much time with much consideration preparing our writings. Our writings contain many selections prepared to impress people with the truth. Now we may simply come to them, not merely to read them, but to speak them in a living way in fellowship. In a meeting in which we speak in this way, people will surely receive the riches of Christ. Recently a co-worker among us testified that in every place that he served, the most difficult thing for him to do was to give a message in the regular meeting on the Lord's Day morning. As the Lord's Day approached, he began to suffer by preparing his message. He had to go to many books to try to select some portions and put them together. All of us, though, have the riches in a condensed form as our rich "groceries." What we need is simply to learn how to "cook." Moreover, these groceries are inexhaustible; they can be used again and again.

According to 1 Corinthians 14:26, however, we should not need to have any printed material (other than psalms, hymns, and spiritual songs) to use in the meetings to help us speak. But all of us are used to relying on something in the meetings from our old way of practice. If I am used to walking with a cane and you suddenly take it away, I will not be able to walk. Temporarily, I still need a cane to rely on until I am able to walk without it. I once had tuberculosis, and it took two and a half years for me to be fully healed. During my sickness, I could not walk without something or someone to help me. We have to realize that we have been crippled by the traditional and unscriptural practice of Christianity. Many of us cannot "walk by ourselves." If the speaker is suddenly taken away from our meetings without anything to replace him, that will be hard. Thus, we may temporarily use the *Life Lessons*, the *Truth Lessons*, the Life-study Messages, or some other spiritual books with weight. We should not use them in the way of one person speaking or some persons reading but in the way of everyone speaking. We can use these materials by speaking them corporately. The meeting should be opened up for everyone to speak. In the long run, we all will get used to speaking. Eventually, we will not need a cane, that is, the printed material, in our regular church meetings.

We may use a "cane," such as the *Life Lessons*, the *Truth Lessons*, or the Life-study Messages to help us at the present time. But I warned the church in Taipei that we must avoid something—if we use such a cane, this can build up a bad habit. We may rely on it too much, and then it could never be taken away. While we are walking with the cane, we also have to learn how to walk without it. Sometimes we need to walk without the cane. If we get tired we may use the cane again to rest. Gradually, we must learn and be fully strengthened to walk without the cane until we no longer need it.

CHAPTER ELEVEN

HOW TO TAKE CARE
OF THE HOME MEETINGS
AND SMALL GROUP MEETINGS

Scripture Reading: Acts 2:46-47; 5:42

In this chapter we want to see how to take care of the
home meetings and small group meetings.

AVOIDING THE PREACHING OR TEACHING
OF THE PASTOR OR PREACHER TYPE

Whenever we attend a home meeting or a small group
meeting, we should avoid the preaching or teaching of the
pastor or preacher type. This means that we should not
behave ourselves as a preacher or a pastor. Do not make
your preaching in the type of a preacher, and do not make
your teaching in the type of a pastor. When we go to the
home meetings, we should be only in the type of what we
are, that is, a brother or a sister. This is not easy for a
person who has been a preacher or a pastor for a number
of years. When this person speaks, he may have the tone of
a preacher. Among the preachers in Christianity there are
different types. The Baptists, Presbyterians, and Episcopa-
lians have different types of preachers. Whenever a
Pentecostal preacher speaks, he does not need to tell others
that he is a Pentecostal. His way of speaking and his tone
make it clear that he is a Pentecostal preacher. In the
Lord's recovery all of us have to be common Christians. We
are simply brothers and sisters.

AVOIDING ACTIVITY OF THE LEADER TYPE

The leader type is mainly among us in the Lord's
recovery. Basically speaking, we do not have the pastor or
preacher type, but we do have the leader type. When
certain brothers speak in the meetings, most of us realize
that they are leaders in the local churches. When a brother

is in the leadership for a certain amount of time, he may build up a type. It is also possible for us to speak in the type of our national or cultural background. A Chinese, Japanese, or Korean brother may speak in the type of China, Japan, or Korea. We in the Lord's recovery must learn to come out of all kinds of types. We need to speak only as a brother or a sister.

Not Doing Everything in the Meeting but Leading the New Ones to Partake of the Meeting

In the home meetings and small group meetings, we must learn the skill not to do everything in the meeting but to lead the new ones to partake of the meeting. We need to be consulting persons when we go to the home meetings. The new ones need to be impressed that the meeting in their home is their meeting. We should tell them that it is not our meeting and that we are not coming to hold our meeting. We are coming to help them have their meeting.

If we go into someone else's home and the family does not know how to cook, we must remember that the kitchen is not ours. We should not cook for them, but we should teach them how to cook. We should help them to do all the cooking. If we feel that we are the experts, we may not allow anyone to do anything. Instead, we may do everything for everybody. The daughter of a mother who is an expert in cooking may not know how to cook well because she has been replaced by her mother. Since the mother is an expert in cooking, she may not let the daughter cook that much. This is the leader type. The leader type does everything for everyone. In the practical service of the church, the leader type may not allow anyone else to clean the restrooms or vacuum the floor. His attitude is—"You don't know how to do this. I know, so let me do it." These leaders do everything. In everything, they are the experts. To them, the others do not know how to do things. Only they know how. Others among us, instead of being leaders, are managers. They take the pretense that they are the "overseers." They are the superintendents watching how others do things.

I have two concerns about your going to the home meetings. One concern is that you will go in the type of a leader, and the other concern is that you will go in the type of a manager. Both are wrong. If both of these types are wrong, how should we behave ourselves? It seems that if we do anything, it is wrong. It also seems that if we do not do anything, that is wrong. If we speak, we speak wrongly. If we do not speak, that is also wrong. Since this is the case, we may feel that we do not need to go to the home meetings or small group gatherings. But to do this is even more wrong. Then what shall we do?

We need to go to the cross. Christ has dealt with all the negative things on the cross, and through His death on the cross, He has released the divine life within Him into us so that we could become His many members which constitute His Body. When we are experiencing the cross, nothing of us remains. Whatever we have, whatever we are, whatever we can do, and whatever we have accomplished should all go to the cross. Nothing of us should be left. The cross takes away everything negative and releases the divine life. When we go to a home meeting or a small group meeting, we should hold an attitude that everything of us should be crossed out. Only one thing should be released through us and out of us—the divine life. I do not mean that we should not act or do anything in the meeting. But we should not do anything in our natural way, by our natural life, and with our natural strength. We should be in fear and trembling that we would offend the Lord by doing anything with our natural strength. Anything that is natural, that is not holy or separated, and anything that we do by our natural strength should be crossed out.

Not Replacing the New Ones but Leading Them to Bear the Responsibilities of the Meeting

Do not replace the new ones, but lead them to bear the responsibilities of the meeting. Lead the new ones to do everything in the meeting. During the initial stage of the first three or four weeks of meeting with the new ones, it might be awkward because many of them have never been in a Christian meeting. They do not know how to pray, how to speak the word of God, or how to sing a hymn. Thus, you have to teach and instruct them like a mother teaching her children to speak or to walk. You have to consider all the new ones as little babes.

In the past we did not help the new ones that much because we did everything for them. We merely charged them to come to the meetings, and we let them observe the meetings. That way was not so profitable or life-giving. Rather, that way somewhat annulled and deadened people. To some extent it also kept people away from the meetings. We have found the secret to having remaining fruit. To have remaining fruit, we must bring the meeting to the new ones' homes. We should not ask them to come to a meeting, but we should bring a meeting to their homes and help them to carry out a meeting in their homes. We need to impress them that the meeting is not our meeting but their meeting.

ALWAYS FELLOWSHIPPING WITH THE NEW ONES IN THE INITIAL STAGE ABOUT HOW TO MEET

We should always fellowship with the new ones in the initial stage about how to meet. We do not need to have a formal program for the home meetings and small group meetings. In the initial stage of meeting with the new believers for the first one or two months, you may stop in the middle of the meeting to have a little talk. Because there are only three to five people in a home meeting, it is easy to stop the meeting and talk a little bit. Then the meeting can resume. In one meeting, we may have to stop three or four times in the initial stage. Otherwise, we will make ourselves the pastors, and the new ones in our home meetings will be our audience like a congregation in Christianity. The meeting should always be carried on in a conversational way. Do not make it so formal or legal. Sometimes you may stop the meeting for three minutes to fellowship in order to guide them, lead them, and bring them into the real practice of meeting. From the very beginning of their Christian life, we must give them the impression that the Christian meetings are gatherings in which every attendant participates.

For the first three terms of the full-time training in Taipei, we did not instruct the trainees to bring the newly baptized ones to the regular church meetings because at that time, the church meetings were still somewhat in the old way. Once the new ones are brought to a meeting with a large congregation and a good speaker, they will be damaged and it will be hard to change their concept. Good mothers know that it is wise to keep their children away from wrong things and sinful things. Once a child sees some wrong, bad, sinful things, it is really hard to wash away the impression. Thus, it is profitable to keep the newly baptized ones meeting in their homes according to the scriptural way so that they acquire a taste for this way. All the children who are raised in Japan have the Japanese taste. If they come to live in the United States, it is hard for them to get rid of their taste. Likewise, if the new ones are brought up in the new way, they will not have a taste for any other way.

RENDERING SOME SHORT TEACHINGS
OF THE CRUCIAL THINGS TO THE NEW ONES
IN THE FELLOWSHIP WITH THEM SPONTANEOUSLY

When you teach the new ones, do not give them the sensation that you are now going to teach them. Rather, render some short teachings of the crucial things to the new ones spontaneously. As you are talking to them, you can insert some teaching. Spontaneously you may open the Bible to 1 Corinthians 14:26 and ask them to read it. Then you can say that this verse tells us that when we Christians come together, each one has something. You may ask the three-year-old girl of the family, "Do you have something?" She may say, "Yes, I have a little song." Then you can say, "Sing it to us." Do not take care of your teaching at that time. Always give them the opportunity to function. This is why the home meeting should not have a prearranged program. We need to take every opportunity to train the new ones to function.

When some of the saints have gone to visit the home meetings, they have gone with a prearranged program. When they entered the home, the little girl may have been singing. Then they told the little girl to stop and sit down so that they could carry out their prearranged program. This is not only very poor but also a killing. Do not stop her singing, but utilize her singing to start the meeting. If you take care of this principle, you will learn a lot.

After the little girl finishes her singing, the mother may ask you what the Passover is in the book of Exodus. Do not tell her that this is too deep for her and that we had better not touch it. This kills the meeting. Even if they ask about the New Jerusalem, you should not tell them that it is too deep for them. Talk with them about the New Jerusalem. The seeking new ones can pick up any new term. It may be hard for us because we are too old, too conservative, and too filled up. We may not be poor in our spirit. Instead we may be overloaded with old concepts and past experiences. Some of the brothers may not understand a certain revelation from the Word even after it is shared a number of times. But it is easy for the new ones who are seeking and simple to receive any new thought from the Word. It is amazing how little children are able to learn a language without formal instruction and without a dictionary. Within a short time they know what the words *mommy* and *daddy* mean and are able to say them.

In the home meetings, the new ones will follow whatever we say. They do not question and critically discern everything that is said. Many of us, however, have become accustomed to the doctrines in the Scriptures and are too full in our spirit. The Lord Jesus said, "Blessed are the poor in spirit" (Matt. 5:3) because the scribes and Pharisees were filled with the traditions and practices of Judaism. There was no emptiness, space, or capacity in them for the Lord's new teaching. This does not mean that we should have a poor spirit but that we should be poor *in* our spirit. We need to be emptied and unloaded in our spirit to receive the new things, the things of the kingdom of the heavens.

HELPING THE NEW ONES TO READ THE BIBLE DAILY AND USE IT FOR THEIR SHARINGS IN THE MEETING

We should also help the new ones to read the Bible daily and use it for their sharings in the meetings. There are two ways for us to help the new ones read the Bible. We may teach them in a formal way, but this is a killing way. Instead we should teach them in a spontaneous way in our talk, our fellowship, with them. If we help them in a spontaneous and informal way, they will begin to read the Bible daily. When we see them after a couple of days, we can informally check with them to see if they are reading the Bible. By talking to them, we can find out whether they have read the Bible or not. In the home meetings we should not do anything formal or legal.

HELPING THE NEW ONES TO CALL, SPEAK, OR SING A HYMN

We should help the new ones to call, speak, or sing a hymn without any formality. We should set the example by calling a hymn first, but we should do it in a wise, proper, and living way. Otherwise, our calling can offend people. We should set up a proper pattern for them, and then lead them into this practice.

HELPING THE NEW ONES TO PRAY, NOT ONLY IN THE MEETINGS BUT ALSO IN THEIR DAILY LIFE

You need to help the new ones to pray, not only in the meetings but also in their daily life. Again, you have to carry out this kind of teaching in a spontaneous way. Do not exercise yourself as a teacher who is teaching them something crucial. That is wrong.

HELPING THE NEW ONES TO FOLLOW THE LORD'S ANOINTING WITHIN THEM AND THE FLOW OF THE MEETING

We also have to help the new ones to follow the Lord's anointing within them and the flow of the meeting. This is something deeper. We still can impart this truth by conversing with them in a spontaneous way. We can tell them that we Christians all have the Lord within us and that the Lord is the anointing. If they do not understand the word *anointing*, we can tell them that this is the same as *oiling*. If a piece of machinery is too dry, we oil it. We can tell them that the Lord is within us, and He is always oiling us to make us run so smoothly. We may even check with them, "Before you called on the name of the Lord, did you ever have this inward feeling?" When they say "no," then we can say, "How about today?" They may say that they do have a good feeling within them now, and they may also tell you that they feel at times that something within is rebuking them. They may say, "I have the feeling that a living person is in me." We can tell them that this is very good and that they now have the real experience of a Christian, but we should not teach them too much.

HELPING EVEN THE CHILDREN
TO CALL, SPEAK, OR SING A HYMN AND
TO QUOTE OR SPEAK THE WORD OF THE BIBLE

In the home meetings, we need to help even the children to call, speak, or sing a hymn and to quote or speak the word of the Bible. Suppose that you have baptized a couple, and they have a nine-year-old boy and a three-year-old girl. If you go to help them have a home meeting, you must train even the three-year-old girl. You can tell her that it is easy for her to call a hymn in the meeting and that it is even easier to sing a hymn. You may say, "You know when you are going to have a home meeting and that some brothers will come to help you. Before we come, you can sing a hymn." If you tell the little girl this, she may be singing when you enter the home. Take her song as the start of the meeting. All the little ones like to sing. You may not need to help the little girl sing a whole verse or stanza of a song. If you can help her to sing one line, she may be happy. The little ones can be a very good help to the home meetings. You also can help them to pray. They can pray a simple prayer such as, "Lord Jesus, You are so good. I love You and I know that You are with me." You can instruct the nine-year-old boy to speak some verses, to read some portion of the Word. In this way all the members of the family participate in the meeting. If we do this week after week with this family, they will accumulate many divine riches.

HOLDING A DEFINITE GOAL FOR THE MEETING AND NEVER LETTING THE MEETING END IN EMPTINESS

You should hold a definite goal for the meeting, and never let the meeting end in emptiness. Go to the meeting with a purpose and keep at least ten minutes of the meeting to fill the new ones with some riches of your purpose. You may stay there for seventy minutes, but you should reserve at least ten minutes for your purpose. We need to consider the way the Lord was on this earth when He talked to people. The four Gospels show us that the Lord talked to people without forms, legalities, or programs. He was always flexible. In any situation and with anyone, a profitable and building up word proceeded out of His mouth. We must learn to talk to people in this way.

Always Trying to Overcome the Deviation in a Pleasant Way

If there is a deviation in the meeting, you should always try to overcome it in a pleasant way. Do not do anything to give people a bad feeling, but always do something in a pleasant way to arrive at your goal, to reach your destination. You are not going to the meeting to have fun with them. You have a purpose to accomplish. You have to reach your destination.

Do not go to someone's home to have a legal, formal meeting. Go there to spend one hour in an informal way. Talk to the new ones in a conversational way and let them say something. As you are meeting with them, one of them may remark that his shoes are too old and that he needs a new pair. Overcome this deviation in a pleasant way. You may say something about their need for a new pair of shoes and then bring the meeting back to the Bible. They will be happy. Do not set up a program with a schedule. If you have a prearranged program, you will have a legalistic attitude to stop any distraction that comes in. If they ask any questions about a different portion of the Bible, you will tell them that it is too deep for them or that it does not fit their situation today. If you have the attitude that only what you are doing is the best, you will kill everything. Go to the homes with no regulation, form, or program. Whatever they do, do it with them. But always hold your purpose and bring them to your goal.

Always Endeavoring to Share
Some Spiritual Reality in Life or in Truth
to Swallow Up the Emptiness

We should always endeavor to share some spiritual reality in life or in truth to swallow up the emptiness. The meeting may have been going on for close to one hour, yet you should still grasp the last ten minutes to minister some reality either in truth or in life. At the end of a meeting, you may raise up the word *redemption*. Then you can speak a little bit about how the Lord died on the cross to accomplish redemption. You can say that we needed redemption because we got lost. We needed to be brought back to God, so the Lord Jesus shed His blood on the cross to take away our sin (John 1:29), to deliver us from the penalty of God's righteousness (John 3:18; 5:24), and to repossess us, accomplishing an eternal redemption for us (Heb. 9:12). Such a short speaking within three minutes ministers a truth to them. In this short time you can impress them with the word *redemption*.

How many among us can give a clear word on the truth concerning the Lord's redemption? In the last thirty years, how many saints have been raised up that can teach others? Most countries on this earth basically practice a similar educational system of kindergarten, elementary school, junior high school, high school, and college. There are also advanced degrees such as a master's degree and a Ph.D. But in the church we have been speaking to the dear saints for years, and not many have come to the full knowledge of the truth. We have to realize that our way in the past was wrong. We need to be brought into the full knowledge of the truth and we also need to bring the new ones into this full knowledge.

FOR THE LONG RUN, USING SOME MATERIALS SUCH AS *LIFE LESSONS*, *TRUTH LESSONS*, THE LIFE-STUDY MESSAGES, OR OTHER SPIRITUAL PUBLICATIONS IN TRUTH OR IN LIFE

For the long run, we need to use some materials such as *Life Lessons*, *Truth Lessons*, the Life-study Messages, or other spiritual publications in truth or in life. We have pointed out that this kind of material can be considered as a "cane" in the initial stage to help us in the meetings. For many years we have been in an old way of meeting in which one person speaks and the rest listen, so we must use a "cane" to help us have a new start. I feel that it is best to use *Life Lessons* first and after a couple of months to use *Truth Lessons* since they are much deeper and richer.

The new ones that we contact will be from different backgrounds. Some who have a high education will like to read things. You can give them *Life Lessons*, but they may feel that this is not sufficient to nourish them. They may want to have some strong food. If you give them *Truth Lessons*, they may feel very good at first because this is deeper. But after a while they may want you to give them something even richer than this. Then you can give them the Life-study Messages. This will satisfy their hunger. Some new ones will like to read to such an extent. Many people are tired of reading the newspapers. They want to read something in a new field. They will be so happy to read the Life-study of Matthew or Genesis. This is not too deep or hard for them because they have such a large capacity.

NOTHING BEING DONE IN LEGALITY OR FORMALITY WITHOUT THE LIVING FLEXIBILITY

You should not do anything in the meetings in legality or formality without the living flexibility. Suppose you have been meeting in a certain home for fifty minutes and a little girl in the family turns on the television. Would you

stop it? Most of us would think that the television being on
would kill the meeting. But I would say that it is better not
to stop it. You have to learn the skill to turn the meeting
back to the Spirit from the television. You can even use
what they are seeing on the television, whether it is good
or bad, to turn the meeting back. Turn the meeting back
wisely. Because we have been drugged with the religious
thought and concept, we like to be legal. We always like to
see things moving in the lane of religion. We all need a
change in this matter.

TAKING CARE OF THE SICKNESSES, SUFFERINGS, TROUBLES, PROBLEMS, AND PHYSICAL NEEDS OF THE NEW ONES IN A BALANCED WAY FOR THEIR BENEFIT, EDIFICATION, AND BUILDING UP

We should take care of the sicknesses, sufferings,
troubles, problems, and physical needs of the new ones in a
balanced way for their benefit, edification, and building
up. Of course, our work is not a work of charity, but a work
to bring God's salvation to the sinners, to impart the
pneumatic Christ into the believing ones, to minister the
divine life to them that they may grow in Christ, and to
build up the local church for the building up of the Body of
Christ. Yet in carrying out such a divine work for the
testimony of Jesus Christ, we have to help the ones who
are under our work in their sicknesses, sufferings, troubles,
problems, and physical needs. We have to learn how to
stand on the Lord's word and exercise our faith and even
lay our hands on the sick ones to heal their sickness. We
have to learn also to share their sufferings, troubles, and
problems by praying for them and doing the best to
comfort them and whatever we can in the capacity that the
Lord gives us to take care of their circumstances. We also
have to help them in their necessities materially after the
Lord's leading and according to the prosperity by which
the Lord has blessed us (Acts 11:29).

CARING FOR THE NEW ONES IN THE SCRIPTURAL WAY TO BEAR REMAINING FRUIT

We should not think that it is hard to help the home

meetings. The Lord told us that His yoke was pleasant and His burden was light (Matt. 11:30). We need to practice taking care of the new ones in the home meetings and small group meetings until we become experts. We have to practice and exercise in a regular way by caring for the new ones in the home meetings week after week. This has to be our habit. We should pick up one or two new ones and consider them as our babes. If we care for them week after week, practicing the points of fellowship in this chapter, we will learn a great deal. By practicing this fellowship, we can keep the new ones living and seeking in the church life. I believe that many of us, as we endeavor in the new way, will even be raised up to train the new ones.

We need to practice constantly, week after week and year after year, to care for the new ones and to raise them up. If we go to visit people about two weekends every three months to get about two new believers, we will have six to eight under our care within a year. Their spiritual education will come from our care. Our meetings with them will become our meeting life. If we are faithful to consistently care for the new ones that we have gained, our fruit will remain. If fifty out of one hundred saints meeting together can practice visiting people according to this fellowship, and two of the six to eight new ones that they have baptized remain, the church can be doubled within one year.

The traditional way of meeting with one speaker cannot meet all the needs of the new ones or of the saints. The specific needs of someone who has been saved for thirty years and another one who has been saved for only three days cannot be met in a large meeting. Our old way of meeting was a deadening way because we met in a way that could not meet the needs of all attendants. The patients in a hospital are not served with the same food or the same medicine. The appropriate food and medicine is dispensed to them according to their condition and need. This is why we need to come back to the way of meeting revealed in the Scriptures.

QUESTIONS AND ANSWERS

Question: How many visiting saints should go to the home meetings?

It is always good to have two or three visiting saints go to the home meetings. It is not as good to go by yourself. For more than three to go would also be good if it is possible. Those who go must bear the burden to "play ball" in the home meeting. You must tell the new ones how they should participate in the meeting by either praying, calling a hymn, or singing. Train and instruct them to join in with your speaking. By your training in meeting after meeting for a couple of months, they will eventually join you in speaking spontaneously. After half a year at the most, they should be completely prepared to participate in the regular meetings.

Question: How can I care for a Spanish-speaking believer, not being able to read the Spanish Life Lessons with her?

This is a difficult problem. There were hundreds of English-speaking saints in our training in Taipei. Some of the Chinese-speaking saints were able to understand English and translate for the English speakers during the preaching of the gospel. This was good. But when we began to take care of the home meetings, the English speakers were not able to do much for the meeting. It was too difficult to translate for them, so we decided not to keep the English speakers in Taipei to help with the home meetings. They could have helped only if they learned Chinese. The problem of different languages, which comes from Babel, is difficult. Some brothers and sisters should do their best to learn Spanish. If there is a will, there is a way. You are not too old for this. Do your best to help the situation.

A WORD OF WARNING

The things that I have fellowshipped with you in this message and in other messages are just some principles. In the practical steps, you still need to pray and look to the Lord for His instant guidance and to follow His leading and guidance in whatever you do and say in any kind of meeting. Please do not make any proposed principles a legality. We must hold a spirit of learning all the time regardless of how much we have learned and experienced. We must be poor all the time in our spirit for receiving further revelation of the Lord.

CHAPTER TWELVE

A CLOSING WORD

The fellowship in this chapter may be considered as advice, not as a charge or a law. We need to exercise much wisdom regarding the way we live our Christian life in our locality after we have seen the light concerning the new way.

NEVER IMPOSING THE NEW WAY ON OTHERS NOR PROMOTING IT

We should neither impose the new way on others nor should we promote it. The best way to carry out the new way is to live as an example. To preach the gospel by visiting people in their homes is altogether scriptural. I do not believe that any of the saints would oppose this. It is possible that some might not be happy to preach the gospel in this way, but we should not impose this on them. It is up to the saints whether or not they would take this way. We trust in the Lord for His doing.

ENDEAVORING TO PRACTICE THE NEW WAY AS THE LORD LEADS ACCORDING TO THE LIMIT OF THE CIRCUMSTANCES

You also need to endeavor to practice the new way as the Lord leads according to the limit of the circumstances. You may be in a local church which does not practice the preaching of the gospel by visiting people in their homes. On the one hand, you should not impose this on others or promote it. On the other hand, you can carry out your burden for this on your own. You can follow the Lord's leading to fellowship with one or two others who would be burdened to go with you to preach the gospel according to the God-ordained way. The Lord will surely lead you to some sons of peace.

In the old way, we were inviting the people, the "fish,"

to come to us, and they would not answer our invitation. That was the reason we did not gain many people in the past. But in the new way we are going to the fish, and we have the assurance in the Lord that we can gain some. If you can gain one new one every three months, you will gain four in a year. This is a good number. But you have to consider how many new ones you and the other saints in your locality are able to take care of. If six in a locality of only fifteen saints are burdened to preach the gospel by visiting people, they can gain twenty to thirty new ones in a year. Actually, if they went out every week they could gain more, but I do not think that this is wise. If we deliver many babies and are not able to care for them, this is not good. Thus, we have to apportion our manpower and our time. The best way for us to take is to gain one or two new ones every three months. Then we will reap some for each of the four seasons. As we take care of them they will grow, and after a year they will be raised up to do what we are doing in the gospel service to the Lord.

If we take this way quietly without promoting it or imposing it on anyone, we will not offend anyone or stir up different opinions. We must do our best not to stir up any turmoil, debate, or argument. The saints will not oppose or criticize you if you preach the gospel by visiting people and set up weekly home meetings with the new ones that you gain. If the church in your locality does not practice the new way, you should do your best to attend the regular meetings of the church, at least on the Lord's Day and if possible the prayer meeting. Then you could reserve one evening a week to either preach the gospel or care for the new ones in their homes. Actually, these home meetings are church meetings in the eyes of God. Do everything in your locality in a loving, nice, and wise way. This is what it means to practice the new way as the Lord leads according to the limit of the circumstances.

EXPRESSING THE LORD'S
HUMILITY AND FORBEARANCE
IN ANY STEP OF THE PRACTICE OF THE NEW WAY

Do everything in humility with forbearance. Never do

anything arrogantly. If we are doing a good work to preach the gospel and raise up the home meetings, we should not have a proud spirit or attitude. If we are living in and with the divine Trinity, none of us can be proud. We always have to be humble and forbearing. In any situation we should not overstep the limit the Lord has given us.

NEVER DESPISING ANYONE
WHO IS NOT POSITIVE FOR THE NEW WAY

Do not make a division or draw a line between who is positive for the new way and who is not. Even in our talk we may say that a certain brother is not for the new way. This is not good and we should never utter anything like this. We should not have the concept that only the saints who are positive for the new way are in the recovery. A brother in a local church who does not agree with the new way is still in the recovery. We who are positive for the new way should not despise or look down on anyone who is not positive. We hope that anyone who does not agree with the scriptural way will not oppose it. Opposing can stir up dissension, and dissension will issue in division. This will be a damage to the Lord's Body. Even a little dissension may kill the blessing of the Lord in the church life.

ALWAYS SUBMITTING YOURSELF
TO THE PRESENT PRACTICE
OF THE LOCAL CHURCH IN YOUR LOCALITY
WITH A POSITIVE, CONSTRUCTIVE, AND BUILDING UP
SPIRIT AND ATTITUDE

Even if the church in your locality does not practice the new way, you still have to submit yourself to the church. If your local church does not practice the new way and you grasp the chance in a meeting to promote it and preach or teach about it, this is not proper and indicates that you are not submitting yourself to the present practice of your local church. What you say depends on the leading of the Spirit. The church in your locality may not practice the new way, yet the spirit, attitude, and atmosphere of the church allows you to fellowship about the new way or give a testimony of your practice of the new way. This is different from promoting, preaching, or teaching. You have to see what the atmosphere in the meeting is and know the attitude and the spirit of the entire church. You may have the sense that it would be good to give a testimony of how you go to visit people, who has been saved, and how the home meetings have helped the new ones. If the atmosphere in the meeting and the spirit and attitude of the church is against this, do not give such a testimony. If the church in your locality does not like to practice according to the scriptural way, submit yourself to their present practice. Even if the church does not like anyone to say anything about the new way, do not say it in a meeting. This does not mean that you cannot talk in your home with the saints. You have the liberty to fellowship with some of the saints in their homes, but do this with a pure motive. Do not have the attitude that since the church is opposing the new way, you will do something secretly to tear down and overthrow the present practice and bring in the new way. This is altogether not good. The Lord does not carry out things in this way.

NEVER DEBATING, ARGUING, OR FIGHTING WITH ANYONE CONCERNING THE NEW WAY BUT CARRYING THE NEW WAY OUT IN A LIVING AND BUILDING UP WAY ACCORDING TO THE LORD'S INSTANT LEADING AND ARRANGEMENT

Once you sense that an argument is rising up, you should stop what you are saying. If five saints are gathered together in a home and two or three of them are opposing, do not talk about the new way. Under the Lord's sovereign arrangement, these opposing ones may leave. The others might be stirred up by the Lord to ask you some questions about your practice of preaching the gospel by visiting people in their homes. Then you can give them a report about what the Lord has been doing, and they will receive some help. We do not need to fight or struggle for anything. We realize the Lord's new way is profitable, scriptural, and workable, so we practice it without promoting. Yet if there is the opportunity, we can fellowship

with the saints and leave the result in the hands of the
Lord. We should never debate, argue, or fight with anyone
concerning the new way, but we should carry the new way
out in a living and building up way according to the Lord's
instant leading and arrangement.

AVOIDING ANY KIND OF DIVISIVE WORD OR DEED
IN KEEPING THE ONENESS OF THE BODY OF CHRIST
WITH A SWEET HARMONY

Sometimes some of the brothers who were so positive
for the new way spoke with a divisive tone. This is unwise
and not good. We should avoid and reject anything that
would even build up a tendency toward division. Our words
and our deeds could be considered by others to be divisive.
We must be wise and take care of the oneness of the Body
of Christ with a sweet harmony. How can there be
harmony between a group of people, when some of them
are positive for the scriptural way and some are not? It
seems that there is a kind of disharmony that is already
existing. But to keep the oneness of the Body of Christ with
a sweet harmony depends on us. By our behavior,
speaking, and actions we can adjust the situation and
recover the harmony. We are brothers with the same faith,
and we are in the church life in the same recovery. This is
our base for oneness. We are harmonious for the one
purpose of having the Lord's recovery to keep the testimony
of the oneness of the Body of Christ. We should not expect
that we can all be the same in everything. Therefore, we
should not try to unify the situation.

ENDEAVORING TO FUNCTION IN ALL THE MEETINGS
OF THE LOCAL CHURCH IN YOUR LOCALITY
ACCORDING TO THE FLOW OF THE PRESENT PRACTICE
OF YOUR LOCAL CHURCH

Some of the younger saints may have been trained in
the new way, but when they returned to a church that did
not practice the new way, they would not function. They
attended the church meetings in a cold way. This is wrong.
As long as you attend a certain meeting, you have to go
along with the practice of that meeting. You must

endeavor to function, not according to your preference but according to the present flow in the meeting. Go on with the saints to show them that you are really one with the Lord's Body in your locality. As long as what is going on is not idolatrous, divisive, or sinful, you must endeavor to function in all the meetings of the local church in your locality according to the flow of the present practice of your local church.

EXERCISING PREVAILING PRAYERS FOR THE LORD'S NEW MOVE AND FOR ALL THE CHURCHES WITH ALL THE SAINTS TO BE GRACED WITH THE HEAVENLY VISION AND THE BOUNTIFUL SUPPLY OF THE SPIRIT

We need to exercise prevailing prayers for the Lord's new move and for all the churches with all the saints to be graced with the heavenly vision and the bountiful supply of the Spirit. We must realize that there is an old traditional way of meeting and serving existing on this earth among the Lord's children. We have already pointed out that it is hard to change something habitual. It would be hard for someone who is used to eating with a fork to switch to eating with chopsticks. The traditional way of meeting and serving is nearly a two thousand-year-old habit. If we try to change this habit in an unwise and quick way, we will stir up much unhappiness. The old way has been built up in Christianity for centuries, and we have it with us to some extent in the Lord's recovery. We have to expect that some will feel unhappy when we want to take away the old way and replace it with the new way. Thus, we have to pray for ourselves and for all the saints that we may see the heavenly vision.

When I decided to make this turn in 1984 to bring in the new way, I realized the hardship that was involved. I also realized that it would be very, very hard to have a new start. When Brother Nee began to fellowship concerning the scriptural way about fifty years ago, we realized then the difficulty involved in carrying it out because of the strong habit built up to meet and to serve in the traditional way. After reconsidering and studying the New Testament, we believe that we have received a vision from the Lord concerning the scriptural way of meeting and serving for the building up of the Body of Christ. Related to the preaching of the gospel in the new way, I would not say that visiting people in their homes is the unique way to preach the gospel, but I have to say that it is the best way, the most prevailing way, the most effective way to bring people to Christ. This vision has burdened me. We have to pray that the Lord would work out something. Whenever the Lord has something to do, He needs His people to cooperate with Him through prayer. We need to pray that all the churches with all the saints would have the heavenly vision and the bountiful supply of the Spirit. Then the saints will join the new way with a heavenly vision by the bountiful supply of the Spirit.

KEEPING FELLOWSHIP
WITH THE CHURCHES AND THE SAINTS
IN THE CONCERN OF THE LORD'S NEW MOVE

We should not be cut off or kept apart from the churches and the saints. We need to keep fellowship with the churches and the saints in the concern of the Lord's new move. We should have much fellowship with one another. We have to fellowship with the churches in Australia. We need to have some communication with the saints in New Zealand. The church in Chicago publishes a newsletter with testimonies concerning the effectiveness of the Lord's new way. This is very good. One testimony in this newsletter tells of a Catholic priest who some brothers met as they were visiting people in their homes with the gospel. This Catholic priest prayed with the brothers and was baptized. He left Catholicism and is now a good brother meeting with the local church. I hope that many churches could publish something to let the saints in other countries and continents know how the Lord is moving in their localities. This may nourish, support, and contribute some help to all the saints, even to the saints outside of us in the denominations.